"In the center of the gleaming copper tray was a large oval dish filled with fried beans and eggs. On one side, hot loaves of flat bread were piled. On the other side were arranged small plates with cheese, pickled lemons, and peppers, as well as salt and cayenne and black pepper. The brothers' bellies were aflame with hunger…"

NAGUIB MAHFOUZ, *PALACE WALK*

CRAZY WATER, PICKLED LEMONS

DIANA HENRY

CRAZY WATER, PICKLED LEMONS

Enchanting dishes
from the Middle East,
the Mediterranean,
and North Africa

photographs by JASON LOWE

To Ted, with love

Crazy Water, Pickled Lemons
by Diana Henry

An Hachette UK Company
www.hachette.co.uk

First published in Great Britain in
2002 by Mitchell Beazley, an imprint
of Octopus Publishing Group Ltd,
Carmelite House, 50 Victoria
Embankment, London EC4Y 0DZ
www.octopusbooksusa.com

First published in North America in
2006
This edition published in 2016

Distributed in the US by Hachette
Book Group, 1290 Avenue of the
Americas, 4th and 5th Floors, New
York, NY 10020

Distributed in Canada by Canadian
Manda Group, 664 Annette St.,
Toronto, Ontario, Canada M6S 2C8

ISBN: 978 1 78472 157 2

Printed and bound in China

10 9 8 7 6 5 4 3 2 1

Commissioning Editor: Rebecca Spry
Executive Art Editor: Yasia Williams
Design: Miranda Harvey
Home economy: Angela Boggiano
Editors: Susan Fleming and Hattie
Ellis
Production: Alex Wiltshire
Index: John Noble

NOTE: In the recipes all eggs are
large unless otherwise stated

I'd like to say a huge "thank you" to the great team that brought this book to life: Angela Boggiano, Susan Fleming, Jamie Grafton, and Fiona Smith, with particular thanks to Jason Lowe for his magical photography and Miranda Harvey for her stunning design. Thanks also to those who have supported and encouraged my work: Leonie Highton, Rosie Stark and Heather Holden-Brown.

For invaluable help in all sorts of ways (expert advice, tasting, testing, translating, and baby-sitting) I'm grateful to Jenny Abbott, Laura Baggio, James Booth-Clibborn, Kate Brownilow, Mehmet Cetin, Lesley Henry, Robin and Joan Henry, Eleanor Logan, Jill Mead, Mitra Powell, Philippa Thomas, Catherine Trippett, and Hugh Fearnley-Whittingstall. Thanks also to the cooks and food-lovers who kindly shared recipes, let me roam around their kitchens and taught me a thing or two: Corrado Constanzo, ice cream-maker extraordinaire from Noto, Sicily; Giuseppe Peppe from *Ristorante da Peppe* in Trapani, Sicily; Jean-Paul Bou Antoun and Ziad Sawaya of *Noura* in London; Hamid Janzemin and Mansour Abdi of *Alounak* in London; Abdel and Frances Boukraa from *Adam's Café* in London; James Hamill from *The Hive Honey Shop*. I'm also indebted to Claudia Roden, whose wonderful, evocative work has inspired me both as a cook and a writer.

Crazy Water, Pickled Lemons could never have been written without the help and encouragement of my husband, Iain, and my friend Briony Fletcher; I am so grateful to them both. Lastly, I owe a huge debt to my editor, Rebecca Spry, whose enthusiasm surpasses even my own, and my good friend Hattie Ellis, who encouraged me to write in the first place and lovingly read every word of this book as it was put together.

Grateful acknowledgment is made for permission to reprint excerpts from the following copyrighted works: *The Second Sex* by Simone de Beauvoir, translated by HM Parshley; *Midnight in Sicily* © Peter Robb, 1996; *Palace Walk* by Naguib Mahfouz, published by Doubleday, all reproduced by permission of Random House US; *Fruits of the Earth* (*Les nourritures terrestres*) by André Gide, translated by Dorothy Bussy, reproduced with permission of Editions Gallimard, Paris; *Les Liaisons Culinaires* by Andreas Staikos © Agra/Stavros Petsopoulos, 1997. English translation © Anne-Marie Stanton-Ife, 2000, reproduced with permission of the Harvill Press; *Two Towns in Provence* by M.F.K. Fisher, reproduced by kind permission of Lescher, New York; 'The Olive Trees' from *Antonio Machado: Selected Poems*, translated by Alan S. Trueblood, Cambridge, Mass. Reprinted by permission of Harvard University Press, © 1982 by the President and Fellows of Harvard College. *Dreams of Tresspass: Tales of a Harem Girlhood* by Fatima Mernissi, © 1994 by Fatima Mernissi, reprinted by permission of Perseus Books. *The Wine Dark Sea* by Leonardo Sciascia reprinted by kind permission of New York Review Books. *The Letters of Katherine Mansfield* and *The Journals of Katherine Mansfield*, edited by John Middleton Murray, reprinted by permission of Constable and Robinson Publishing Ltd. *The Tassajara Bread Book* by Edward Espe Brown © 1970 by the Chief Priest, Zen Center, San Francisco. Revisions © 1986 by Edward Espe Brown. Reprinted by arrangement with Shambhala Publications, Inc., Boston, www.shambhala.com. *Travels in Persia 1673-1677* by Sir John Chardin reprinted by arrangement with Dover Publications Inc. 'Walnut' by Abu Bakr Muhammad ibn al-Qutiyya from *Poems of Arab Andalusia*, translated by Cola Franzen. Copyright © 1989 Cola Franzen. Reprinted by permission of City Lights Books. *The Sultan's Seraglio* by Ottaviano Bon, reproduced by permission of Saqi Books. *The Unprejudiced Palate* by Angelo Pellegrini reproduced by permission of Angela Owen Pellegrini. 'Figs', from *The Complete Poems of DH Lawrence*, and extracts from *Sea and Sardinia* reproduced by permission of Laurence Pollinger Ltd and the Estate of Frieda Lawrence Ravagli. *The Voices of Marrakech* (ISBN 071452580) by Elias Canetti, reproduced by permission of Marion Boyars Publishers. *Four Meals* by Meir Shalev, reproduced by permission of Canongate Books. 'A Lemon' by Pablo Neruda, translated by Ben Belitt from *Selected Poems of Pablo Neruda*. English translation © 1961 by Ben Belitt. Used by permission of Grove/Atlantic, Inc. Excerpts from *The Debt to Pleasure* by John Lanchester, © 1996 by John Lanchester. Reprinted by permission of Henry Holt and Company, LLC. *Prospero's Cell* by Lawrence Durrell, reprinted by permission of Faber and Faber. 'Sixteen Haiku' from *Complete Poems by George Seferis*, translated by Edmund Keeley and Philip Sherrard © 1967 Princeton University Press, 1995 renewed PUP/1995 revised edition. Reproduced by permission of the publishers. 'You Hated Spain' from *Birthday Letters* by Ted Hughes, reprinted by kind permission of the author's estate and Farrar Straus and Giroux. 'Namaz', by Arash Saedinia from *A World Between: Poems, Short Stories and Essays by Iranian-Americans*, published by George Braziller. Reproduced by kind permission of the author. 'A Propos de Nice' by Adrian Henri, © Adrian Henri, 2000. First published in *HQ Poetry Magazine* and reproduced by permission of the author c/o Rogers, Coleridge and White Ltd, 20 Powis Mews, London W11 1JN. Extracts and recipe from *Honey from a Weed* by Patience Gray, published by Prospect Books, reproduced by kind permission of the author. Recipe from *The Chez Panisse Menu Cookbook* by Alice Waters, reproduced by arrangement with the author and A.M. Heath Ltd. Adapted recipe from *The Independent Cook* by Jeremy Round, printed by permission of A.M. Heath Ltd. Recipe from *The Complete Middle East Cookbook* by Tess Mallos, reproduced by permission of Grub Street. Extract and recipe from *A New Book of Middle Eastern Food* by Claudia Roden reprinted by kind permission of the author. Thanks to Fox Publishing for allowing me to reproduce work which appeared in *Food and Travel*.

CONTENTS

INTRODUCTION

CRAZY WATER, PICKLED LEMONS

I came to live in London in my early twenties. I moved into a tiny basement apartment, in the north of the city, that had a kitchenette with a cream carpet that was soon covered in stains. Everything had to be stored in one tall cupboard, which made it impossible to get at my saucepans without being attacked by an old upright vacuum cleaner. But any shortcomings were made up for by what I found around me. At the end of my road there was a green-fronted Turkish grocery which, alongside toilet rolls and tea bags, sold bottles of flower water, pails of flavored olives, and jars of sesame paste. A short trip to the Edgeware Road led to the heart of London's Arab community, where among the hubbly-bubbly pipes and mint-tea drinking I discovered sacks of pistachios and sour, shrivelled fruits called barberries. There were trays of Turkish delight, flavored with lemon and orange blossom as well as rose water and, in the autumn, I could come home from the local street market with bags of honeyed quinces.

I bought Claudia Roden's *New Book of Middle Eastern Food* and curled up with it on the sofa when I got home from work in the evenings. I may have been looking out at London rain, orange streetlights, and the darkening feet of passers-by above me, but the writing – and the recipes – took me to Cairo. In my imagination I went for afternoon tea with Roden's aunts in a place of tinkling glasses, tiny spoons, and silver dishes of pure color, where the smell of musk, ambergris, and jasmine hung in the air. It was like reading an adult version of *The Arabian Nights*, except that now the treasure troves of jewels were bursting with ripe figs, sticky dates, and glass phials of flower water. I was already a keen cook, but now, in my basement apartment, a whole world opened up for me, and it wasn't just one of new flavors. With this book, and these ingredients, I could travel while standing still.

As I cooked more, discovered new recipes and tried this and that ethnic restaurant, I realized that there were particular foods and dishes I thought of as magical. There were ingredients whose properties were so unusual or whose provenance so exotic that they could, like the unicorn, have been invented by writers of myths: leathery pomegranates, their insides bursting with ruby seeds; saffron, the dried stigmas of crocus flowers gathered before dawn in Spanish fields. There were dishes which looked quite ordinary but which had undergone such a transformation in cooking that I couldn't understand how they worked, such as Middle Eastern orange cake, made with unpeeled oranges, boiled, puréed, mixed with eggs, sugar, and flour and baked to a citrus-like moistness; or Persian ice cream, with its chewiness and rose-scented flavour, the product of flower water, powdered orchid root, and ground mastic.

Then there were dishes whose poetry came from their evocative names or stories, as well as from their taste. Think of Ice in Heaven: a Middle Eastern milk pudding of rose-perfumed ground rice; Pearl Divers' Rice: honey-sweetened rice from Bahrain to be eaten with lamb, so-called because its high sugar content was thought to help pearl divers stay under the water for longer; or the Crazy Water of the title: an Italian dish of seabass poached in a salty, garlicky broth, cooked by the fishermen of the Amalfi coast. Other dishes just seemed magical by being out of the ordinary, bold in their simplicity or simply for the apparent dissonance of their ingredients, such as Catalan Stuffed Chicken with Honey and Quince Aioli.

Senses, as well as tastes, are locked up in food. The clear, perfumed stillness of a bottle of flower water, the sexy, velvety skin of a fig, the sunburned blood color of a jar of cayenne… Our love of foods has as much to do with what they represent as with what they taste like.

Nearly all the ingredients and dishes which, for me, have this otherworldly quality are from Spain, Portugal, the southern regions of France and Italy, the Middle East, and North Africa. They are Mediterranean dishes, but many of them had been stamped with an Arab or Persian influence. This is aromatic, perfumed or sweet-and-sour food – food that is marked with the decorativeness of the culture from which it comes. Many of these dishes evolved when the Arabs took their love of fruits, nuts, spices, perfumes, and sheer sensuality into the countries they conquered.

You'll also find Ottoman influences, recipes from the Berber tradition, distinctive Catalan dishes whose evolution is impossible to divine, and some Provençal and southern Italian recipes. The only prerequisite in putting this book together was that every dish should have a kind of magic.

The recipes have been garnered from cooks I've met, many of them living away from their homeland; adaptations of recipes from other food writers; dishes I've created; and recipes given to me by chefs around the world. I hate fusion food – but authenticity does not have to mean rigidity, or cooking would never develop – and so I have even adapted traditional dishes. Many of the Middle Eastern dessert recipes are less sweet than the originals, simply because I prefer them with less sugar; other recipes have been adjusted so that they're quicker to make.

The ingredients I have found so exhilarating are now widely available, but this doesn't mean they have lost their charm. I love my forays to Middle Eastern shops and the thrill of picking up foods in foreign markets, but I'm glad that I can get most of them without going too far. The specialness is in the food itself. It excites me to see a jar of pickled lemons wedged in between the ketchup and the cornflakes in my kitchen cabinet, a bottle of pomegranate molasses hiding behind the marmalade, or a scarlet and sky-blue box of Arabic script nudged up against the bold English lettering on a bottle of Worcestershire sauce. It is a cabinet full of possibilities. It offers me the chance to experience the otherness of places by cooking and eating, to go on journeys with my taste buds and my mind. With food, you don't have buy an airline ticket or don a backpack; the magic of the exotic is there, right beside the everyday stuff, for you to bring into your kitchen.

THE SPICE TRAIL

CARDAMOM, CHILI, CINNAMON, CUMIN, GINGER, CILANTRO, PIMENTON, AND SAFFRON

Spices embody our love of the exotic. Stored in little packets, glass jars, boxes or tins, every ingredient is rendered special. They are small postcards from the edges of the world, synonymous with the East and Arabia even when, as with cumin and coriander, their provenance is actually the Mediterranean. Empires have been built on the back of them, wars waged over them, and world-altering explorations undertaken to find them. They have always enchanted.

Two of the most alluring are saffron and cardamom: cardamom because its taste is so elusive – the dishes it flavors seem like a ghost has walked through them; saffron for those blood-red threads that turn whole dishes to gold, bleeding yolk-yellow streaks over creamy chicken and milky-white yogurt. It seems extraordinary that anyone thought of cooking with the stigmas of a flower, the crocus, but nearly everything about saffron is otherworldly: that the stigmas have to be picked from mauve-ribboned fields on the morning they appear, before sun, rain or wind can damage them; that the blossoms, separated from the red filaments, turn the pickers' hands blue with their juice; that women with decades of experience dry the stigmas over heat using no gauge other than their nose and eyes. Yet saffron must be used sparingly, since it has an inherent bitterness, a pungency of mushrooms and smoke. It has to perfume food rather than suffuse it – a good job, since it is by far the most expensive spice.

The Persians, with their love of jeweled food, adore saffron, and color handfuls of rice saffron-yellow before scattering them over dishes of white rice grains. In Moroccan and Spanish dishes, saffron haunts tomato sauces and tomato-based fish soups, adding a subtle, smoky spiciness; the most famous Spanish rice dishes, *paella* and *arroz con pollo*, seem to have been invented for saffron; along with cardamom, it is the best spice for adding to creamy dishes. The slight bitter-sweetness of a saffron sauce is perfect with shellfish, and a cream sauce infused with saffron and cardamom makes a decadent partner for chicken.

Saffron seems at its most extravagant in desserts – you feel like you're cooking with gold – but here you must be very restrained or its flavor will jar. Try a tad in a delicate ice cream, a smidgen in a pistachio-studded rice pudding, a few threads in a pan of honey-poached apricots, or infuse some strands in cream to make a saffron crème brûlée with poached plums or apricots hidden in the bottom.

Cardamom needs a light touch, too. Cardamom seeds, when released from their pods and ground, smell of roses and licorice. When I'm cooking with cardamom I visualize it as a misty vapor wafting through food. (Cleopatra actually did turn cardamom to smoke, burning it in her chambers during Mark Antony's visits.) I always want its flavor to be stronger, and yet, if it is, the effect is destroyed. An excess of cardamom tastes like a drugstore. Cardamom's a flavor best yearned for. Add it in whispers.

Cardamom's perfume easily infuses cream – use it in rice pudding, white or dark chocolate mousse, and to make heavenly ice cream. Try it in citrus syrups too – make one with orange juice, honey and cardamom for bathing orange slices, or even just for drizzling on ice cream or milky desserts. Coffee is another good partner – hardly surprising when you think that half the cardamom produced in the world ends up in Arab coffee. The spice is usually ground into the drink, but the Bedouin tribes of North Africa place cracked pods in the spout of the coffee pot itself. A few ground pods added to coffee cake or coffee ice cream subtly change their whole character.

In the same way that saffron's exoticness is increased when added to sweet dishes, cinnamon's is increased when added to savory ones. Cinnamon, along with allspice, is *the* spice for those little meatballs of minced lamb, *kofta*, which you find all over the Middle East. Cinnamon really brings out the sweetness of lamb, making *kofta* the perfect partner for bowls of earthy hummus and tart thick yogurt. I put a pinch in my otherwise perfectly English shepherd's pie, and make a delightful savory-sweet Greek-inspired dish of minced lamb with chopped dates and cinnamon encased in filo pastry.

When it comes to desserts, I could live without cinnamon, though I like the Moroccan habit of sprinkling it on flower water-perfumed oranges. Cinnamon's effect on sweetness is cloying, its image too cute. I'd rather have sassy ginger, the Lucille Ball of the spice world, pepping up my sugar rushes. Plucky, assertive and, when fresh, full of tongue-prickling juice, ginger – with its tight beige skin, veined like slub silk – is beautiful. It comes in many forms: there's fresh root ginger (not a root at all but a rhizome, or underground stem of the plant); ground powder; slices pickled in vinegar, and tender nuggets preserved in syrup. Preserved, ginger's a great pantry standby for chopping up and mixing into creamy rhubarb, plum or apple fools. Make ginger syrup by simmering slices of fresh ginger in a sugar syrup until the required piquancy is reached. Enhance the syrup's exoticism with fresh lime, star anise or chopped lemon grass and you have a fragrant sauce for sliced fresh mango or melon, or ice cream. Ginger syrup is a good medium in which to poach apricots, too, or knead a little of the powdered spice into nuggets of marzipan to stuff pears or plums for baking.

In savory dishes we associate ginger with Chinese, Thai, and Indian food. But Moroccans love it, too; they always use it in the powdered form, which is hotter and more warming without the tangy freshness of the root. Ginger goes into rich *tajines* of meat and fruit, where, alongside saffron, cinnamon, cumin, and cayenne, it mellows to a warm, sweet glow. Moroccans also use ginger with fish, especially shad, which is rubbed with ginger and filled with ginger-and-rice-stuffed dates.

Chilies are a minefield, and not just for your taste buds. They come in so many forms and strengths: fresh, dried, powdered, and flaked; from long, tapering green ones, just mild enough to pickle for the *mezze* table, to the lethal tiny red tongues of fire called bird's eyes. There are several hundred varieties, all part of the great capsicum family. Many of them developed in the countries to which they spread — paprika in Hungary and *pimentón* in Spain, for example. I used to get confused over all those red powders — cayenne, paprika, and *pimentón* — and would use them interchangeably. But it's simple: they are the ground powders of different varieties of capsicum. Cayenne pepper is usually ground from a single variety and is hot, about seven on a scale of one to ten. Paprika (which developed in Hungary after the Turks took chilies there) and the Spanish *pimentón* are ground from several chilies and come in both hot and sweet forms. Cayenne and paprika are used throughout the Middle East, although more for their underlying fruitiness than for heat. For burn, Algerians and Tunisians make a biting red-chili paste called *harissa* — a must for adding to couscous broth.

Pimentón is Spanish paprika and comes in two forms. *Pimentón de la Vera* is smoked, and has a sweet, woody, smoked-bacon flavor; it's great added to mayonnaise to be eaten with seafood, mixed with olive oil and lemon to make a marinade for chicken, or sprinkled on olive oil-roasted potato wedges. Regular *pimentón* is sun-dried and not that different from Hungarian paprika.

I always keep a jar of dried chili flakes handy. Once they're heated in a little olive oil, they give any dish a shot in the arm. When there's not much food in the refrigerator, sauté a few sliced garlic cloves, add a sprinkling of chili flakes, a bunch of finely chopped parsley, a squeeze of lemon and some salt, toss with warm spaghetti, and you have a great heat-speckled supper to eat in front of the TV.

Cumin has none of the beauty of chilies, nor the intrigue of ginger, but it's my favorite spice. A real workhorse, its coarse, ridged seeds smell like earth and life: fresh sweat, sex, dust, maleness. Walk through an Arab market anywhere and cumin, mingled with orange flower water, fresh cilantro and mint, is the underlying odor. It seems to come from people's skin as well as the stalls.

Cumin's earthiness goes well with the most basic of ingredients — lentils, fried potatoes, and pulses. Hummus is nothing without it. It can provide a supporting bass note above which more shrill spices sing, but it more often dominates. In Morocco it's used as a kind of pepper; little dishes of salt and ground cumin are offered with grilled chicken and lamb or hard-boiled eggs. In Egypt you can buy a street snack of eggs with little paper cones of *dukka* — a mixture of salt, pepper, roughly ground roasted cumin, coriander and sesame seeds, and perhaps also hazelnuts — in which to dip them. Try quail eggs with *dukka*. Or mix butter with crushed garlic, cayenne, and freshly ground cumin to make a spice paste for the Moroccan lamb dish, *mechoui*. In Morocco they cook huge sides of spiced lamb on a spit; at home, simply get a big shoulder of lamb, make incisions all over it, and rub the spiced butter into the holes in the meat. Cook long and slow in the oven until meltingly tender and serve with Arab bread, quarters of lemon, and little bowls of salt and cumin. It's a feast fit for a *caliph*.

In Europe, only the Spanish and Portuguese use cumin, and sparingly at that, but they do great things with it. Try marinating chicken joints in honey, cumin, garlic, and lemon before roasting for a good sour-sweet bolt of Catalonia, or frying potatoes with a mixture of cumin and smoky *pimentón*.

Coriander seeds, with their echoes of orange rind and toasted hazelnuts, complement cumin. I love the sound of freshly toasted coriander and cumin seeds — and they *should* be toasted and freshly ground as their oils are volatile — cracking and splintering as you pound them. Throw a last-minute dose of them, with a handful of fresh cilantro, into simmering lentils for depth and freshness.

The only rules with spices are to buy them in small quantities so that you don't harbor tasteless jars of old powder, and to grind freshly the ones which most benefit from it: cardamom, coriander, and cumin. After that, each bit of sorcery you perform with them will help you to know them better.

MOROCCAN CHICKEN WITH TOMATOES AND SAFFRON-HONEY JAM

My adaptation of a Moroccan dish. There the result is usually much sweeter and can be more elaborate. In a wonderful Moroccan restaurant called La Mansouria, in Paris, I've eaten a version of this dish which even contained pounded rose petals (though, to be honest, you couldn't tell). Moroccons also serve the sauce on its own as part of their mezze.

Recipes should be guides rather than instructions set in stone, but in this case do what the recipe says; reduce the sauce until it is really jammy.

serves 4

3¾ lb chicken,
    jointed into 8 pieces

salt and pepper

olive oil

1 large onion, roughly chopped

3 garlic cloves, crushed

2½ tsp ground cinnamon

1½ tsp ginger

1¾ lb tomatoes,
    roughly chopped

1¼ cups (10fl oz) chicken
    stock or water

½ tsp saffron threads

5 tbsp honey

1 tsp orange flower water

1 oz slivered
    almonds, toasted

a small bunch of cilantro,
    roughly chopped

1 Season the chicken pieces and quickly brown them all over in 2 tbsp of olive oil. Set the chicken aside and cook the onion in the same pan until soft and just coloring. Add the garlic, cinnamon, and ginger and cook, stirring, for about a minute. Tip in the tomatoes, mix everything together well, turn the heat down, and cook for another 5 minutes or so, stirring from time to time.

2 Boil the water or stock and dissolve the saffron in it. Pour this over the vegetables and bring the whole thing up to the boil. Set the chicken pieces on top, together with any juices that have leached out of them, and spoon the liquid over them. Turn down to a gentle simmer, cover and cook until the chicken is tender – it should take about 30 minutes, but check after 25.

3 Remove the chicken pieces, set them aside, cover, and keep warm. Now bring the juices to the boil and simmer until well-reduced to a kind of "cream" – it shouldn't be at all sloppy. Add the honey and continue to cook until well-reduced and jam-like. Check the seasoning and add the orange-flower water. Put the chicken pieces back and warm them through in the sauce.

4 Serve scattered with the toasted almonds and chopped cilantro, with couscous or flatbread on the side.

"Yours are the rarest of spices;

nard and saffron, calamus, and cinnamon, and

all the trees that bear incense; myrrh and

aloes, and all the subtlest of aromas"

THE SONG OF SONGS

SPANISH SAUSAGES AND *MIGAS*

A brilliant Andalusian breakfast dish, or indeed any-time-of-the-day dish, that really zaps the taste buds. Its flavor reminds me of those Mexican breakfast dishes — hashes of peppers, sausage, hot spice and eggs wrapped in a floury tortilla — but here the starch comes in the form of fried bread cubes or migas. *The word "crouton" just doesn't begin to describe* migas. *Cooked slowly so that they color on the outside while remaining fluffy on the inside, they are the core joy of this dish. Don't reach for any of that cotton-ball and cardboard-tasting type of bread; you need the well-flavored, coarse, country kind for* migas.

serves 2 greedy people

3 tbsp water

3 tbsp milk

salt and pepper

13oz stale white bread,
    crusts removed, and torn
    into irregular chunks

8 tbsp olive oil

6oz chorizo, cut into
thick rounds

¼ lb pancetta, cut into
    meaty chunks

1 tsp *pimentón de la vera*
    (sweet, smoked
    Spanish paprika)

(¼ tsp ground cumin

1 onion, finely chopped

1 red and 1 green pepper,
    deseeded and chopped

2 garlic cloves, finely chopped

4 eggs

24 seedless white grapes,
    skinned, to serve (optional)

1 Mix the water and milk together and add a little salt. Soak the bread in this mixture for about half an hour. Heat 1 tbsp of the olive oil in a pan and cook the chorizo and pancetta until well-colored. Lift out with a slotted spoon and set aside. Put another 2 tbsp olive oil into the pan, heat, then add the bread with the *pimentón*, cumin, and freshly ground pepper. Cook the bread very gently over a low heat for about 25 minutes. It's important to do this really slowly so that the insides stay soft and fluffy while the outsides become golden.

2 Heat another tablespoon of oil in another frying pan and sauté the onion and peppers until soft and just beginning to brown. It will take about 15 minutes. Add the garlic and the cooked pancetta and chorizo, and cook for a further couple of minutes, until everything is hot.

3 Add the onion mixture to the *migas* and stir everything around. Quickly fry four eggs in olive oil and dish these up on top of the *migas* mixture. The Spanish also like to serve it surrounded by peeled grapes (it may sound unusual, but it works) — you do whatever you feel like.

"Concerning the spices of Arabia, let no more be said. The whole country is scented with them, and exhales an odor marvelously sweet."

HERODOTUS

KUSHARY

A warm, autumnal rice dish flecked with dark-brown onions, kushary is an Egyptian staple whose name means "messy mix"— you find hole-in-the-wall take-outs and traveling carts all over Cairo selling it by the bowlful. It provides a bolt of energy and protein and is considered to be a no-frills fuel food. Served with chopped cucumber and seasoned yogurt, I think kushary's a great vegetarian soother, but it's also a good side dish. As well as with tomato sauce, kushary is often served with raw onions that have been left to marinate in wine vinegar. Leave out the macaroni and the tomato sauce and you have megadarra, *another Egyptian pilaf.*

serves 4-6

4oz long-grain rice

5oz brown lentils

8 tbsp olive oil

1 onion, roughly chopped

3oz small macaroni

1 tsp ground cumin

1¾ cups (14fl oz) chicken or
   vegetable stock or water

salt and pepper

2 onions, cut in
   half-moon shapes

FOR THE SAUCE

1 x 14oz can of tomatoes
   in thick juice

½ onion, finely chopped

1 celery stick, finely chopped

2 tbsp olive oil

1 tsp harissa (*see* p19)

2 tsp soft brown sugar

1 Make the spicy tomato sauce by putting all the ingredients in a saucepan, stirring, and bringing everything to the boil. Turn the heat down low and let the sauce simmer for 25 minutes, stirring from time to time. You can purée the sauce in a food processor to get a smoother texture once it's cool, or leave it as it is.

2 Rinse the rice until the water runs clear, then soak it in water for 2 hours. Wash the lentils and soak them in water for half an hour. Cover the lentils with fresh water and cook for 15 minutes.

3 Heat 2 tbsp of the olive oil in a pan and sauté the chopped onion until browned, but not burned.

4 Cook the pasta in water until *al dente,* then drain and sauté in 1 tbsp of olive oil until the edges start to become colored. Set the macaroni aside, too.

5 Drain the lentils and the rice and heat 2 tbsp olive oil in a heavy-bottomed saucepan. Stir the lentils and rice round in this and add the cumin and the cooked onion. Cook for about a minute, then add the stock or water, some salt, and pepper. Bring to the boil, then turn down to a simmer. Let the rice and lentil mixture cook, uncovered, for about 20 minutes, by which time the liquid will have been absorbed. Then stir in the pasta, cover, and leave on a low heat for 5 minutes so that the bottom becomes browned.

6 Heat the rest of the oil until it is very hot. Brown the remaining onions in the rice mixture, breaking up the little crispy bits from the bottom of the pan. Check the seasoning and serve with the spicy tomato sauce.

JEWELED PERSIAN RICE

Iranians have turned the cooking of rice into an art form, and this gold-splattered orange and saffron-sweet dish is at the pinnacle of their achievements. It takes some effort, but you get to weave a bit of magic, transforming humble foods into a dish of sparkling exoticism.

serves 4

10½ oz basmati rice

salt and pepper

2 oranges

2 carrots

a good 1oz blanched almonds,
    cut into slivers

½ tsp saffron threads

1½ tsp dried rose petals

½ tsp ground cinnamon

seeds of 10 cardamom
    pods, crushed

1 tbsp vegetable oil

1½ oz unsalted butter

1 tbsp granulated sugar

a good 1oz pistachios,
    very roughly chopped

a good 1oz raisins,
    soaked in warm water
    and drained

a good 1oz dried barberries

FOR THE TAHDEEG

4 tbsp vegetable oil

a good 1oz unsalted butter

TO SERVE

1½ oz butter (optional)

1 Wash the rice, cover with lightly salted water, and soak for 3 hours.

2 Remove the peel from the oranges, leaving the pith behind, and cut it into julienne strips. Cover with cold water, bring to the boil, and cook for 2 minutes, then drain and rinse. Peel the carrots and cut them into narrow strips, about 3¼ inches long. Toast the almonds in a dry pan and soak the saffron in about 2 tbsp of just-boiled water. Mix the rose petals, cinnamon, and cardamom together.

3 Heat the oil and butter in a frying pan and sauté the carrot for about 4 minutes until it is softening. Add the sugar and the orange peel and cook for a further minute. Pour on the saffron water and add the almonds, pistachios, and dried fruits. Remove from the heat and set aside.

4 Bring a large pan of salted water to the boil; drain and rinse the rice and pour it into the boiling water. Bring the rice back to the boil and cook fairly vigorously for no more than 3 minutes, then test it – the grains should be beginning to soften on the outside but remain firm in the center. Keep testing until it gets to the right stage. Drain the rice and rinse in tepid water.

5 Now you need to create the *tahdeeg* – the all-important crust that forms at the bottom of the rice. Heat the fats in a large pan and, when sizzling, spoon on a layer of rice. Separate a quarter of the carrot and saffron mix and put it aside. Layer the remainder with the rice, sprinkling the rice on gently and seasoning with the spice mix, salt, and pepper as you go.

6 Make three holes in the rice with a spoon handle, wrap the saucepan lid in a dish towel, ensuring the ends of the cloth are folded over the top, and cover the pan. Leave on a high heat for 4 minutes to get the steam going, then cook on a low heat for 15 minutes. Quickly lift the lid and test if the rice is cooked, but don't stir it.

7 Once the rice has cooked, put the saucepan onto a cold surface; this will make it easier to remove the crust later. Spoon the rice onto a hot serving platter and garnish with the reserved saffron and carrot mix. The crusty bit is traditionally served separately, but I break it up and mix it in with everything else. If you want a sheen, melt the last bit of butter and pour it over the rice.

B'STILLA

Even the appearance of b'stilla, *with its diamond pattern of confectioner's sugar and cinnamon echoing Moroccan latticework, suggests hidden secrets — a flavor of the unexpected. It's a sumptuous dish — a layering of poultry (traditionally pigeon), cilantro-infused eggs, almonds, cinnamon, sugar, and pastry. In Morocco it's properly made with onion-skin-thin* warka *pastry, but filo is a fine substitute. There are different versions; some include preserved lemon or orange-flower water, and some have no sugar at all, but try this more common sweet one first.*

serves 8 as an appetizer,
4-6 as a lunch with salad

2 cups (16fl oz) chicken stock

2 onions, or 1 very large one,
   very finely chopped

½ tsp ground ginger

½ cinnamon stick

½ tsp saffron threads,
   infused in 2 tbsp hot
   water for 15 minutes

a small bunch of parsley,
   roughly chopped

salt and pepper

1 guinea fowl

2½ oz sliced almonds, toasted

1½ tbsp confectioner's sugar,
   plus extra for dusting

½ tsp ground cinnamon,
   plus extra for dusting

2oz butter

8 sheets filo pastry

5 eggs, beaten

a medium bunch of cilantro,
   roughly chopped

3 tbsp lemon juice

1 Bring the chicken stock to the boil and add the onions, ginger, cinnamon, saffron, half the parsley, and some salt and pepper. Put the guinea fowl into the stock, turn the heat down, cover, and simmer for 45 minutes.

2 Take the guinea fowl out of the stock and, when it's cool enough to handle, take the flesh off the bones, leaving the skin behind. Boil the stock left in the pan until it's reduced to 1 cup. Remove the cinnamon.

3 In a small bowl, mix the almonds with the sugar and the ground cinnamon. Preheat the oven to 400°F, and put a metal baking sheet into it.

4 Melt the butter and line a eight-inch springform pan with the filo pastry. Put in one sheet at a time, turning the pan so that the pastry hangs over the sides all the way around. Use five sheets for the bottom, brushing with the melted butter between each sheet.

5 Gently heat the stock, add the eggs, and cook until the eggs have scrambled slightly but are not firm and dry. Stir in the cilantro, the rest of the parsley, and the lemon juice.

6 Put the guinea fowl on top of the filo pastry in the pan and pour on the egg mixture, followed by the almond mixture. Put the remaining filo on top and, brushing with butter, seal the pie by pulling the overhanging sides onto the top. Brush the surface with butter, slide it onto the heated baking sheet, and bake for 20 minutes.

7 Remove the pie from the springform pan and invert it onto the baking sheet, brush the top with more melted butter and return it to the oven to cook for another 15 minutes. Sift confectioner's sugar over the top and make a lattice pattern with ground cinnamon.

HARISSA

A fiery red chili paste from North Africa, usually served with couscous, which can just about take the roof off your mouth. Use it in marinades, or slightly diluted with a little water and olive oil as a hot accompaniment for spicy roasts.

makes 4oz

2 tsp each of caraway,
    coriander, and cumin seeds

2oz fresh red chilies, deseeded

2oz dried guajillo chilies,
    soaked in warm water,
    drained and deseeded
    (reserve the soaking liquid)

6 garlic cloves

leaves from a small
    bunch of cilantro

a good squeeze of lemon juice

5 tbsp olive oil

½ tsp salt

1 Toast the caraway, coriander, and cumin seeds together in a dry pan. Heat them for 3-4 minutes until they start to really release their fragrances. Pound the spices in a mortar and pestle.

2 Put the spices together with all the other *harissa* ingredients in a food processor and purée. You want to end up with a thick but not solid paste, so add a little of the chili soaking liquid to get the right texture.

"The winner of the race would receive a prize made by the last one to cross the finish line: an enormous pastilla, *the most delicious of all of Allah's varied foods. At once a pastry and a meal,* pastilla *is sweet and salty, made of pigeon meat with nuts, sugar and cinnamon. Oh!* Pastilla *crunches when you munch on it, and you have to eat it with delicate gestures — no rushing, please, or else you will get sugar and cinnamon all over your face."*

FATIMA MERNISSI, *DREAMS OF TRESPASS,*
TALES OF A HAREM GIRLHOOD

HARISSA-MARINATED LAMB WITH SPICED MASHED VEGETABLES AND CINNAMON ONIONS

A Middle Eastern spin on meat and potatoes. You can use commercial harissa, *though it doesn't have the vibrancy of the homemade stuff.*

serves 4

8 chunky lamb chops or
   4 lamb steaks

salt and pepper

FOR THE MARINADE

8 tbsp olive oil

2½ tbsp *harissa* (*see* p19)

3 garlic cloves, crushed

juice of ½ lemon

a good handful of
   mint leaves, torn

FOR THE
MASHED VEGETABLES

1lb potatoes, peeled

1lb 7oz parsnips, peeled
   and chopped

5 tbsp heavy cream

3½ oz butter

½ tsp ground cinnamon

¾ tsp cayenne

¼ cup (2fl oz) milk

FOR THE ONIONS

2 onions, very finely sliced

½ oz butter

1½ tsp olive oil

½ tsp ground cinnamon

½ tsp *harissa* (*see* p19)

a good squeeze of lemon juice

a small bunch of cilantro,
   roughly chopped

1 Mix the ingredients for the marinade together, and put the lamb chops into it, turning them over to make sure they get well-coated. Cover, put in the refrigerator, and leave to marinate for anything from 1½ hours to overnight, turning them every so often.

2 For the mash, boil the potatoes and the parsnips separately until they are soft. Drain the potatoes and keep them in the saucepan they were cooked in. Put a clean, scrunched-up dish towel on top of them, and cover. Let these sit for a few minutes on a very low heat – this just helps to dry out the potatoes a bit, and will give you better mashed vegetables. Drain the parsnips and purée them together with the cream in a food processor. Mash the potatoes and put them through a *mouli-légumes* or potato ricer if you have the time and inclination – it is worth it, but we've got to be realistic here.

3 Melt the butter in a saucepan and briefly cook the spices. Add the potato and parsnip and beat everything together. Warm the milk and add that too, stirring as you do so. Season. Let the mashed vegetables sit with the lid on if you don't want to serve the dish immediately – you can reheat it gently if you need to just before serving.

4 Make the onion topping by frying the onions in the butter and oil until golden. Turn up the heat and quickly allow the onions to brown so that some of them become crisp. Add the cinnamon, *harissa*, salt, pepper, lemon juice, and cilantro, and cook for another minute.

5 Heat a griddle for the chops. Salt them at the last minute and then cook them on a high heat until browned on both sides but pink in the middle.

6 Put the warm mashed vegetables into a heated bowl, put the mound of onions on top, and serve with the chops.

LECHE MERENGADA

Great — an ice cream that has an intriguing taste and texture and yet is made without a custard base, so there's no danger of ending up with scrambled eggs. Leche merengada actually means "meringued milk", and that's all it is: whisked egg whites, milk, and cream. It's so simple you'll be surprised that it works. Much more refreshing than custard-based ice cream, it's a staple of Spanish bars in the summer. In fact, you can go completely hip and Hispanic and give everyone a blanco y negro *— that's* Leche merengada *with iced espresso poured over it. Very chic.*

serves 8

2 cups (16fl oz) milk

⅝ cup (5fl oz) heavy cream

5½ oz superfine sugar

peeled rind from 1 lemon,
 white pith removed

1 cinnamon stick

1 tbsp brandy

3 egg whites

ground cinnamon, for serving

1 Put the milk, cream, 3½oz of the sugar, the lemon rind, and cinnamon stick into a saucepan. Bring to just under the boil. Remove from the heat and let the mixture infuse for about 40 minutes. Strain the mixture through a sieve and add the brandy.

2 Whisk the egg whites with the remaining sugar until stiff. Fold this into the cream and milk mixture — it will seem impossible to incorporate, but don't worry: it will all get beaten together during the freezing process. Either still-freeze, beating the mixture from time to time in a food processor or with an electric hand whisk, or churn in an ice-cream machine.

3 Sprinkle with cinnamon before serving.

"...the records of English spice consumption show a heroic commitment to (especially) overrated cinnamon ... aromatic allspice; flashy paprika ... beds-i'-the-east-are-soft cumin ... risky cardamom; unmistakable caraway; lurid turmeric — I could go on."

JOHN LANCHESTER, *THE DEBT TO PLEASURE*

LADIES' NAVELS WITH CARDAMOM, ROSE SYRUP, AND BERRIES

These little Turkish doughnuts don't come with all the extras in their country of origin, but I think it's a lovely combination. I've given unusually exacting instructions, but if you're not careful you'll end up with something nearer ladies' backsides than ladies' navels – I know whereof I speak.

serves 4-6

FOR THE SYRUP

1 cup (8fl oz) water

10½oz superfine sugar

seeds from 3 cardamom pods

a good squeeze of lime juice

2 tbsp rose water

FOR THE LADIES' NAVELS

3½oz all-purpose flour, sifted

1oz superfine sugar, sifted

1 cup water

2oz butter

2 small eggs, beaten

groundnut (peanut) oil
    for shaping and deep-frying

TO SERVE

a handful of fragrant rose
    petals or chopped pistachios

Greek yogurt

berries (choose from
    raspberries, blueberries
    or blackberries

1 For the syrup, put the water into a small pan with the sugar and the seeds from the cardamom pods. Heat slowly, stirring to help the sugar dissolve. When the sugar has melted, bring the syrup up to the boil and let it cook for 7 minutes. Leave to cool. Strain and add the lime juice and rose water.

2 For the navels, put the water, sugar and butter into a saucepan. Bring to the boil slowly – both the butter and sugar should melt before the water boils. As soon as it boils, add in the flour, stirring all the time. Quickly bring everything together. The dough will eventually amalgamate, leaving the sides of the saucepan. Set aside to cool.

3 Gradually add the eggs to the dough. The dough will separate and you will despair of ever getting it to come together again, but it will – just beat it like crazy with your wooden spoon.

4 Oil a few cookie sheets and your hands and scoop up walnut-sized pieces of the dough. Roll these into balls and put them on to the oiled sheets. Use your little finger to make a hole right through the center of each ball.

5 Heat about six inches of oil in the bottom of a large saucepan and, when it's warm, add half of the navels. Raise the temperature until the oil is at a steady 400°F and cook the navels for 10 minutes, turning frequently to make sure they brown evenly. They should be deep golden and the center should be cooked. You may have to practice with the first couple until you get the temperature right – this quantity allows for a few disasters.

6 Drain the navels on kitchen paper, then immediately dunk them in the sugar syrup and put them on a plate. In Turkey they are left to steep for 10 minutes, but I think this makes them much too sweet. Do the same with the rest of the navels, then sprinkle them either with rose petals – torn or cut into strips – or chopped pistachios. Serve with thick yogurt and berries.

"...when he opened the heavy door, the warm swallows of rosemary and wine, olive and garlic soared out of there, and their wings fluttered over my nose until I grew dizzy with pleasure"

MEIR SHALEV, *FOUR MEALS*

FRAGRANCE OF THE EARTH

LAVENDER, ROSEMARY, THYME, AND OREGANO

I am not, by choice, an early riser. My husband jokes that the only thing that gets me out of bed willingly is the smell of fresh coffee and hot croissants. But it's different when I'm on vacation in Provence. There, as soon as it starts getting light, you can find me with my nose stuck out the bedroom window. I might go back to bed afterwards, but it's worth disturbing even the deepest of sleeps to take in that 6am scent of grass and herbs as they begin to warm. Of all the smells in the world – wild strawberries; bacon frying; the sweet, bready scent of a baby's head – this is my favorite.

A mixture of savory, lavender, wild thyme, and rosemary, the aroma could not be described as "sweet". This is the *garrigue*, a sun-baked scrubland of poor soil, harsh light and olive trees. The smell is pungent: pine needles, pepper, camphor, and citrus. I like it best in the morning because it's softer, promising hot weather and herb-marinated chops for lunch. By midday, when every footfall releases its smell and your head is pulsing in time with the cicadas, you'll be almost drunk with it and half asleep (not just a fanciful notion; oil of lavender is a relaxant, so it isn't only the heat that makes you drowsy).

With hardy herbs we are firmly in Europe, land of rosemary-stuffed lamb and oregano-topped pizzas. But that doesn't mean they're dull. These feisty little plants have the potential to deliver dishes every bit as exotic as those from Africa and the Middle East. You do have to look at them again, though. Take rosemary, for example. For years I've been throwing it onto focaccia, or into the roasting pan with chicken, garlic, and potatoes. A meaty fish such as monkfish can stand up to it, and I love to use the stalks as a natural skewer for scallops or chunks of lamb. When it's abundant – and great bushes of it seem to lurk round every suburban corner – it's a treat thrown onto the coals of a barbecue or even, in winter, on to the fire. Like the Italians, I love rosemary and use it a lot; what more could I want of it?

Then I came across a *chocolatier* in Provence, Joël Durand in St-Rémy, who uses rosemary to flavor dark chocolate; a weird combination, you might think, but it works. This led me to try rosemary with other sweet things and I found that its pine-scented herbiness was wonderful in all sorts of wintry desserts. Put a sprig in the poaching liquid for pears or plums; scatter rosemary leaves over an upside-down apple cake; infuse the herb in a custard to make an ice cream for any of these fruits, or in cider for a syllabub, or – my favorite of all – in a citrus syrup for a winter salad of blood oranges, navel oranges, and ruby-red grapefruit. I get a real thrill out of seeing a sprig of rosemary floating, unexpectedly, in this bowl of sweet, glowing slices.

The Med may be rosemary's home, but this herb will survive the chill of a colder climate, and even the worst gardener can't kill it. It's always there at the back door, its sprigs standing like miniature pine trees. Value its steadfastness, and take advantage of it.

Rosemary can, however, be a bit of a brute; too much of it and your dish will taste of the pharmacy (British food writer Elizabeth David rather tartly commented that there was no place for it in her kitchen except in a vase), but with a light hand this herb can grace much more than the odd leg of lamb.

I'm not going to suggest that you put oregano in your desserts, but it's still worth getting to know it better. Oregano is the wild herb from which the milder marjoram was bred, and it's the one most likely to be left for years on the shelves of a spice rack, turning to dust in its jar, misunderstood and underrated. I would throw the odd bit of oregano into tomato sauce or on top of a pizza (it's the classic herb for pizza Neapolitan), but I didn't really appreciate it until I bought some Greek oregano, or *rigani* as it's called there. A stronger, sharper version of Italian oregano, the Greek stuff is rich, resinous, and peppery, permeating to the core of whatever it coats and able to withstand chilies, olives, capers, anchovies, and the rigors of flames and long, slow cooking.

Rigani means "joy of the mountains", and cushions of it soften hillsides all over Greece. Dried and sold in fuzzy green bunches, *rigani* is rubbed into meaty fish, roasts, and kabobs, added to pots of bubbling tomatoes and eggplant and ground into meatballs and soups. It's the bossiest herb in the garden. The great thing is that it's actually better dried than fresh – drying concentrates its flavor rather than subduing it. I keep a big bunch of *rigani* in a tall jar and, on evenings when the supermarket has sold out of every other fresh herb, I can still have a Mediterranean grilling fest.

Sicilians make *salmoriglio* with fresh oregano, mixing the leaves with extra-virgin olive oil, lemon, salt, and pepper to create a vibrant sauce for tuna, swordfish and lamb. In other southern Italian regions oregano joins chili in marinades for chops or chicken – a knockout combination. But remember that any oregano grown away from a burning-hot climate, whether it's fresh or dried, will be much milder in flavor, so taste before using it.

The strength of thyme is also affected by where it's grown. The bunch of wild stuff you buy in a Provençal market, already dried by the sun's glare, is a long way from the thyme in your garden, but both are fragrant with the thymol which gives the herb its distinctive flavor. Thyme isn't the bully that oregano and even rosemary can be, yet it mixes well with both. It can simultaneously imprint its own special flavor and meld well with other ingredients. It can be soft and sweet in a soup of creamy carrots, or tap-dance on grilled shrimp, and it's the only one of these hardier herbs that is gentle enough to go with eggs and cheese. I like it for this – that its fragile, twiggy little body has such pluck and, at the same time, such generosity.

In the past I've nearly always used thyme with other herbs, but lately I've been letting it be its own sweet self. Its oils are volatile when heated, so a final blow of fresh leaves in a dish of braised lamb or grilled chicken just heightens its fragrance.

As far as desserts go, I'd try thyme with anything I'd put rosemary in, as well as with more eggy desserts: baked custards or the French batter dessert *clafoutis*, for example. Thyme's also good in some preserves, such as apple jelly and orange marmalade, and its soft leaves are easily incorporated into bread doughs and cake batters. There are hundreds of varieties of thyme, so you can mess around with the citrus varieties, lemon and orange (good for cakes), or aniseedy caraway thyme (try this in bread).

I have always associated the smell of lavender with my grandmother. On her bathroom window-sill she kept a big bottle of lavender water, using it as both a skin toner and bath scent. Since she had soft, peachy cheeks right into her eighties, it must have worked. (She wasn't alone in this habit, of course; countless other grannies use lavender water and the ancient Romans added sprigs of lavender to their bath water. Indeed, the name "lavender" actually comes from the Latin *lavare* – "to wash"). The image of lavender growing in great purple swathes across the Provençal countryside was firmly stamped over this, making the herb seem less cute. It didn't so much mean bags of potpourri as hot, sweaty afternoons. Adding fragrance, a breath of Provence, and purpleness to food just seemed irresistible. I started to imagine lavender with freshly ground almonds, in cakes or the frangipane of a tart. I tried it in the poaching liquid for apricots, peaches, and cherries, added it to shortbread and *clafoutis*.

The faintest hint of lavender can be achieved by making lavender sugar, blending the flowers and granulated sugar together in a coffee grinder until you have a floral confectioner's sugar. Showers of this can be sifted over fruit-topped meringues or stirred into delicate set custards and mousses, adding a flavor which diners can't quite identify. Lavender and honey ice cream gives the most intense "essence-of-lavender" result; eating pale gold scoops of it with raspberries you can almost hear the midday buzzing of bees, and friends react as if you've cooked with a magic potion – "Lavender ice cream? Oh my God!"

Savories don't have to miss out, either. Lavender actually tastes like a mild version of rosemary with a breath of the floral wreathed around it. I love a lavender, honey, and balsamic marinade for duck or chicken – it always amazes me that those delicate little purple flowers can take on such meaty partners – and a plum and lavender sauce or a savory apple and lavender jelly is great with pork.

Unfortunately, lavender hasn't yet appeared in the herb section of our supermarkets, so you need to grow it, or beg or steal it from a gardener. Obviously, it shouldn't be sprayed with anything, and try and harvest it when the buds are out but not fully open – that's when the flavor is at its most powerful. You can sometimes find dried lavender in the shops, but make sure it can be used for cooking, not throwing in the bath, and replace fresh lavender in recipes with half the amount of dried.

We tend to think much more about basic ingredients – a good chicken, a fresh fish – than the additions. But just as you might deliberate over a plain string of pearls, a pair of gaudy glass earrings or a fine silver chain to go with that little black dress, think about how herbs can create a totally different mood and tone. They are the invaluable accessories of the culinary world – both for everyday wear or for dressing up.

THYME, OREGANO, AND CITRUS-ROASTED POUSSINS

A really easy, gloriously aromatic dish that looks stunning.

serves 4

4 poussins

salt and pepper

4 oranges, skin left on, cut
into large wedges

olive oil

a small bunch of
flat-leaf parsley

FOR THE MARINADE

rind of 1 orange and 1 lime

juice of 4 oranges and 1 lime

6 tbsp balsamic vinegar

½ cup (4fl oz) olive oil

6 garlic cloves, crushed

leaves from about 6 sprigs
of thyme

3 tbsp dried Greek
oregano (*rigani*)

1 Mix all the marinade ingredients together, seasoning with salt and pepper. Put the poussins, breast-side down, into the marinade, cover and refrigerate for a couple of hours or overnight. Move the poussins around every so often so that all the sides get a chance to soak in the marinade.

2 Take the poussins out of the marinade and put them into a roasting pan with the oranges. Drizzle a little extra oil over the oranges and season them. Roast in an oven preheated to 350°F for 50 minutes, spooning the marinade over everything as it cooks.

3 When the poussins are cooked, drain off the pan juices, skim off the fat, and slightly reduce the juices in a saucepan by boiling for a few minutes, until you have something with the consistency of light gravy.

4 Serve the poussins surrounded by the orange wedges and parsley leaves, with the juices on the side.

"During moments of faith and credulity I am almost tempted to believe that what is most necessary in the preparation of distinguished food was preordained to grow with savage fury and to withstand all weather. This is certainly true of rosemary, sage, and thyme."

ANGELO PELLEGRINI, *THE UNPREJUDICED PALATE*

ROAST DUCK WITH HONEY, LAVENDER, AND THYME

Lip-smackingly good and a great summer treat served with new potatoes and green beans. The sauce is little more than a slightly fancy gravy and a breeze to whip up if you have stock in the freezer. You do have to bother to drain the fat off, though, or it burns.

serves 4

1 x 5½ lb duck, giblets
    removed, rinsed
8 tbsp clear honey
2 garlic cloves
3 tbsp brandy
leaves from 6 sprigs
    thyme, chopped
salt and pepper
flowers from 8 sprigs of
    fresh lavender or 4 tsp
    dried lavender

FOR THE SAUCE

2 shallots, finely chopped
1oz butter
¼ cup (2fl oz) white wine
1¼ cup (10fl oz) chicken or
    duck stock
1½ tbsp lavender vinegar,
    or good white-wine vinegar

1 Put the honey and lavender in a small saucepan and gently bring to just below the boil. Remove from the heat and leave to infuse for 2 hours.

2 Make incisions all over the duck. Cut the garlic into slivers and push it into the cuts. Rub the brandy all over the bird and then scatter the chopped thyme over it, pushing some of it into the incisions. Season, cover, and leave for 2 hours or refrigerate overnight.

3 Remove the lavender from the honey by picking out the blossoms or, if you're using dried lavender, reheating and straining it. Reserve 2 tbsp of the honey for the sauce and spoon the rest over the duck.

4 Put the duck on a rack in a roasting pan and cook for 15 minutes in an oven preheated to 425°F. Remove the bird, turn the oven down to 375°F, and drain off the fat. Put the duck back in the oven and roast for a further 1¼ hours, draining off the fat every 20 minutes or so. You will probably need to cover the duck loosely with foil for the last ½ hour – the honey on the skin will caramelize but you don't want it to burn.

5 Make the sauce while the duck is cooking. Sauté the shallots in the butter until soft but not colored. Add the wine and simmer until it is reduced to a couple of tablespoons. Add the stock and reserved honey. Bring to the boil and cook until reduced by about two-thirds. Strain to remove the shallots. Taste and then add the vinegar a bit at a time; it should be a sweet-sour sauce, neither too sickly nor too tart. Season with freshly ground black pepper; it's unlikely to need salt because the stock is so reduced.

6 When the duck is cooked, put it onto a warm platter, cover, and keep it warm to let it rest for 10 minutes. Add any of the juices that leach out to the sauce. Serve the duck with the sauce on the side.

SIMPLE GREEK LAMB

Sunday lunch, Greek-style. This is a throwback to the days when people didn't have their own ovens. Then, dishes were taken to the local baker to be cooked, so they had to be simple and easily transportable, just like this. It's perfect for a weekend lunch, when you're exhausted and want to talk to your guests rather than stand in the kitchen, as it's both delicious and hassle-free.

serves 6

1 x 4lb leg of lamb

juice of 2 lemons

8 tbsp olive oil

1½ tsp dried Greek

oregano (*rigani*)

leaves from 3 sprigs thyme

salt and pepper

4 heads garlic, unpeeled but
    halved, plus 6 peeled cloves

1½lb waxy potatoes

2 medium onions, sliced in
    half-moons

8oz plum tomatoes, quartered

1 cup (8fl oz) dry white wine

1 Make incisions all over the lamb. Mix together the lemon juice, olive oil, oregano, thyme leaves, and seasoning and pour two-thirds of this over the lamb. Massage the marinade into the lamb, making sure that some goes into the slits. Cut the peeled garlic cloves into slivers and push them into all the little holes. Cover and leave the lamb to marinate for as long as you can — anything between an hour and overnight — in the refrigerator. Turn it every so often. Reserve the rest of the marinade.

2 You don't have to peel the potatoes, but you may need to halve or quarter them if they're big. Put the lamb into a roasting dish which will hold all the vegetables as well. Mix the potatoes, onions, tomatoes and heads of garlic with the remaining marinade and put them all round the lamb.

3 Cook everything for 1 hour in an oven preheated to 375°F, basting the meat and turning the vegetables from time to time. Halfway through the cooking time, pour the wine over and around the lamb.

4 When everything is cooked, cover the lamb and vegetables with foil. Insulate the roasting dish with a couple of towels and let the meat rest for 15 minutes.

5 Serve the lamb on a platter surrounded by the vegetables. You don't need anything else except a bowl of green salad.

"Damocles decided to dedicate the entire afternoon to the preparation of divine baked potatoes for his beloved Nana. Nothing special. Just one of the most irresistible, albeit familiar dishes in the Greek culinary repertoire: lamb with roast potatoes. After all, it's not what *you cook, it's how you cook it."*

ANDREAS STAIKOS, *LES LIAISONS CULINAIRES*

LAVENDER, ORANGE, AND ALMOND CAKE

I love the very idea of this cake, never mind its taste. The mixture of lavender flowers with oranges and almonds just reeks of picnics, hot sun and fields of blossom. Making it really lifts your spirits.

serves 8-10

4 tsp dried lavender buds,
 or flowers from 8 sprigs
 fresh lavender

9oz superfine sugar

9oz unsalted butter

juice and finely grated rind of
 2 oranges

4 eggs, beaten

7oz self-rising flour, sifted

2oz blanched almonds,
 freshly ground

FOR THE TOP

10½oz cream or ricotta cheese

2½oz confectioner's sugar

finely grated rind of 1 orange

FOR THE CANDIED PEEL

2 large oranges

3½oz superfine sugar

FOR THE FROSTED
LAVENDER (OPTIONAL)

8 sprigs fresh lavender,
 flowers only

1 egg white, lightly beaten

sifted superfine sugar

1 Put the lavender and sugar in a coffee grinder (or a food processor if you don't have a coffee grinder, though you won't get such a fine powder) and process to a powder. Cream the butter and lavender sugar together until light and fluffy and then add the orange rind and juice and the eggs. Beat until well-combined, adding a spoonful or two of the flour if the mixture begins to look curdled. Fold in the flour and the ground almonds.

2 Pour the batter into an eight-inch) greased and lined springform cake pan and bake in a preheated oven at 375°F for 40 minutes. Test if the cake is cooked by piercing it with a skewer. If the skewer comes out clean it is ready. Let the cake cool in the pan for 15 minutes, then turn it out on to a wire rack.

3 To make the topping, mix the cream or ricotta cheese with the confectioner's sugar and the orange rind. Refrigerate until needed.

4 For the candied peel, use a sharp knife to cut the rind off the oranges in strips. Remove any white pith left on the rind and cut the peel into fine julienne strips, about the length of your little finger. Squeeze the juice from both oranges and make it up to 1 cup with a little water if you need to. Put the juice in a pan with the sugar. Heat gently until the sugar has melted, then add the strips of rind and let them simmer – they need to cook until the liquid has nearly evaporated (about 30 minutes). Scoop the pieces of rind out with a fork and, gently separating them, lay them on a piece of waxed paper to dry.

5 You can only frost fresh lavender. If you want to do this simply brush each sprig with a little egg white, then sprinkle with superfine sugar, covering it well. Set the lavender aside on a cooling rack in a warm place to let it dry and set.

6 Top the cake with the cream cheese or ricotta icing and decorate with the orange zest and the sprigs of frosted lavender.

7 If you can't be bothered with candying and frosting, then use a zester to remove the rind from the oranges and sprinkle it, while still moist, with a little superfine sugar, before scattering it round the border of the cake.

LEMON AND ROSEMARY CAKE

A good bung-it-all-in-together cake, based on UK food writer Sophie Grigson's recipe for a Tunisian almond cake. I always find myself making this on those Sunday afternoons when you want the smell of baking in the house but can't be bothered with too much mess.

serves 8

2oz stale white bread

3½ oz blanched almonds

2 tsp rosemary leaves

7oz superfine sugar

2 tsp baking powder

grated zest of 1 lemon

⅞ cup (7fl oz) olive oil

4 eggs, beaten

FOR THE SYRUP

juice of 2 lemons

½ cup (4fl oz) water

2¼ oz superfine sugar

2 sprigs rosemary

FOR THE GARNISH

confectioner's sugar

1 Put the bread, almonds, and rosemary leaves in a food processor and grind as finely as possible. Combine this mixture in a bowl with the sugar and baking powder. Add the lemon zest, olive oil, and eggs and stir well until everything is amalgamated.

2 Pour the batter into a greased eight-inch springform cake pan. Put it into a cold oven and set the heat to 350°F. Bake for 45-50 minutes, or until the cake is browned and a skewer inserted into the middle comes out clean. Leave in the pan for 5-10 minutes to cool slightly, then turn it out onto a plate.

3 Make the syrup by gently heating all the ingredients together. Stir a little until the sugar has dissolved, then turn the heat up and boil for 5 minutes. Leave the rosemary in the syrup to infuse.

4 Pierce holes in the cake and strain the syrup all over it while it's still warm. Leave the cake to cool. Dust with confectioner's sugar and serve with berries or citrus fruits in syrup and a spoonful of yogurt.

CHOCOLATE AND ROSEMARY SORBET

Intense and slightly bitter, this is one for serious chocolate-lovers. I serve it with folds of heavy cream mixed with sweetened Greek yogurt and handfuls of raspberries.

serves 4-6

2 sprigs rosemary

7oz superfine sugar

2¼ oz cocoa powder

2¼ cups (18fl oz) water

1 Bruise the rosemary – just bash it with the back of a wooden spoon – and put it into a saucepan with the sugar, cocoa powder, and water. Heat gently, stirring a little to help the cocoa and sugar to melt. Bring the liquid up to the boil and boil for 1 minute, stirring occasionally. Take the pan off the heat and leave to cool with the rosemary still in the chocolate syrup.

2 Remove the rosemary and churn the liquid in an ice-cream machine, or still-freeze, beating the mixture a couple of times during the freezing process.

HERB-SCENTED CHOCOLATE TRUFFLES

*In St-Rémy, Provence, Joël Durand makes all kinds of flavored chocolate —
everything from Earl Grey to cardamom. And you can look right into his workshop
through a huge window on the street. These truffles were inspired by his
flavor combinations.*

DARK CHOCOLATE LAVENDER TRUFFLES

makes 20 truffles

5½ fl oz heavy cream

12 sprigs fresh lavender

7oz dark (semi-sweet)
   chocolate

¾ oz unsalted butter

3 tbsp confectioner's
   sugar, sifted

cocoa powder for coating

1 Heat the cream with the lavender sprigs until boiling. Turn off the heat
and let the mixture infuse for 40 minutes. Boil the cream again, then strain
off the lavender and leave the cream to cool a little.

2 Melt the chocolate in a bowl set over a pan of simmering water. The bowl
shouldn't touch the water — you need to melt the chocolate gently. Add the
unsalted butter and let it melt in the warm chocolate, then stir in the sugar
and the cream. Mix well. Remove from the heat.

3 Let the mixture cool, then refrigerate until it is firm enough to handle.
When it's cool, form the chocolate into irregular truffle shapes (they look
better if they are rough rather than perfect balls) and roll in the cocoa
powder. Put them in the refrigerator until you want to serve them and eat
within 48 hours.

4 To be really chic, pour the warm truffle mix onto a flat plate and, when it
is firm and set, make truffle curls by pulling a small ice-cream scoop or
melon baller through the chocolate. Sift all over with cocoa powder to finish.

DARK CHOCOLATE ROSEMARY TRUFFLES

Follow the recipe above, but use 10 sprigs of rosemary instead of
the lavender.

"It's lovely weather — warm, mild.

The air smells of faint, far-off tangerines with

just a touch of nutmeg. On my table there are

cornflowers and jonquils with rosemary sprigs...

How wonderful the earth is."

THE LETTERS OF KATHERINE MANSFIELD,
VOLUME ONE

"Pounding fragrant things — particularly garlic, basil, parsley — is a tremendous antidote to depression. Pounding these things produces an alteration in one's being — from sighing with fatigue to inhaling with pleasure."

PATIENCE GRAY, *HONEY FROM A WEED*

A BOWL OF FRESH HERBS

PARSLEY, CILANTRO, DILL, BASIL, AND MINT

We get so used to employing certain herbs in particular ways: a little sprig of mint imparting an echo of itself to new potatoes; leaves of basil sweetening a plate of vine tomatoes; handfuls of chopped parsley giving a final, celery-like freshness to a long-simmered chicken soup. In fact, it's often impossible to smell these herbs without simultaneously smelling the dishes they so commonly infuse. Like a partner in a comfortable marriage, we begin to see them only in a particular light, or even cease to notice them at all. Then, suddenly, you taste a new dish from a different country using the same old herb and it's like being with a different person. Parsley – great, coarsely chopped mounds of it – when mixed with slivers of onion and abundant lemon juice, is suddenly brash, manfully cutting through the spices of Lebanese lamb *kofta*. Mint finds herself being eaten by the handful with sheep cheese and flatbread as a Persian appetizer. And basil, well she, dancing with her new partners, parsley and cilantro, in a Georgian dish of fish with eggplant and pomegranates, is positively triumphant. "Thought you'd keep me holed up in that little apartment in Genoa?" she seems to jeer. "Well, I've got news for YOU!"

For Middle Eastern dishes you can forget those pathetic little packs of greenery that pass for bunches of herbs in many supermarkets. In the Middle East, herbs aren't just used to perfume or embellish a dish; in many cases they *are* the dish and you have to buy them by the armful. Leaving a Middle Eastern greengrocer's, your head swims with the citric smell of your bouquet of cilantro, or the cleansing scent of a bunch of mint that could see you through a year of mint sauce. It's enough to make you want to roll around in grassy meadows. My God, I always think, am I really going to cook with this much fragrant greenness? What culinary extravagance!

It took just one meal in a Persian restaurant for me to see these soft-leaved flavor enhancers as players in their own right. The classic Iranian appetizer, *sabzi khordan*, was set on our table while we were still looking through the menu. It's nothing more than a bowl of fresh herbs, artlessly thrown together, a slab of feta-like sheep cheese, some radishes, spring onions, and sheets of warm flatbread.

The herb bowl should contain a mixture of tarragon, basil, mint and costmary (which is rather like watercress), though I've been served flat-leaf parsley and cilantro as part of it, too. The idea is that you pick at this tangle, pulling the leaves of basil and tarragon from their stalks and eating them with the bread, radishes, and cheese. The bowl stays on the table throughout the meal in case you want to chew a little mint with your skewered lamb or add a little parsley to your rice. Left thus unadulterated, you taste these herbs as if for the first time. And yes, aniseedy tarragon goes surprisingly well with sheep cheese; mint, eaten leaf-by-leaf instead of as a flavor enhancer in cooking water, zings across your palate; basil, away from its tomato partnership, suddenly tastes of cinnamon.

Iranians, along with other Middle Eastern cooks, use familiar herbs in ways which, to northern European and American sensibilities, are quite unexpected. Take dill, the greenish-blue fronds that you associate with cold northern climes, whose caraway scent flavors Scandinavian cured salmon and Russian borscht. Dill's as big in Iran as it is in Sweden, and there's so much of it in Persian fava bean pilaf that you have trouble seeing the rice. Dill also goes into braised spinach, soups, and herb-laden stews. The Greeks and Turks love dill, too, adding it to rice and bulgar pilafs, or mixing it with ground lamb for *kofta* and with eggs and feta cheese for stuffing filo pies. Further east, in Georgia, dill's stirred, at the last minute, into plum sauce to serve with fried chicken, and sour-cherry pilaf to serve with lamb. Feta, fava beans, lamb and tart red fruits… dill's great with them all.

So for dill there is definitely life beyond *gravlax*, that raw, delightfully thinly sliced cured salmon seasoned with the herb in question. And for parsley there is life beyond chicken soup, because nobody honors parsley like the Lebanese. There, as throughout the Med, parsley is the flat-leafed variety, not the curly one, and it's treated as a salad leaf as well as as a flavoring. The ubiquitous *tabbouleh* is such a parsley-fest that it's difficult to divine that tomato and bulgar wheat lurk there, too. Parsley is also layered with tomatoes, warm rags of pita bread and cucumber to make the Lebanese salad *fattoush*, and the herb finds its way into most of the marinades that imbue meat destined for the Lebanese grill.

In North Africa, huge handfuls of chopped parsley are mixed with black olives, diced red onion, slivers of preserved lemon, and olive oil to make an aggressive salad, and parsley's one of the main ingredients in the Moroccan herb and spice relish known as *chermoula*. Blithely sunbathing with cilantro, cumin, chili, and cinnamon, it's hard to believe that parsley ever soothes us in the creamy embrace of a parsley sauce. But a whole new side of parsley's personality comes to the fore when it co-stars with the eastern flavor of cilantro. Try adding cilantro and parsley together, instead of cilantro by itself, to Moroccan *tajines* of chicken and pickled lemons, or to lamb and apricots, to see just how exotic parsley can be.

Cilantro's a funny one. The most widely used herb in the world – it's used in India, southeast Asia, South America, and the Middle East – people either love it or loathe it. It's been described as "fetid" and "sweaty" and accused of smelling like bedbugs, (its ancient Greek name, *koris*, means "bedbug"), although unless you spend your time sniffing mattresses in insalubrious places, I'm not sure how you'd know.

You don't come across cilantro in European Mediterranean dishes, except in Portuguese cooking. There they stir cilantro into rice, add it to fava beans with bacon, scatter it over fried potatoes, and put it in the salad bowl. But in the Middle East they use it with total abandon, perhaps because its pungent citrus flavor cries out for chili, lemon, and cumin.

On the one hand cilantro can take center stage, puréed with spices, lemon, garlic and oil to make a sauce, or thrown into a bowl for an eastern-tasting salad. But it can also play something of the role that lemon takes, that of flavor enhancer. Cilantro completes a spicy lentil stew, bringing out something that even lemon can't; it pulls together the disparate elements in an Egyptian stuffing of walnuts, pomegranates and garlic; it intensifies the fruitiness of a Georgian blackberry sauce. There are so many flavors that cilantro works well with – cumin, garlic, lemon and lime, ginger, chili, saffron, and sour red fruits – that it can be a good chum as well as the leader of the pack. I like it for that.

Mint, too, can insinuate or look you straight in the eye. Away from the confines of a bowl of English peas, she's pretty determined to jettison the subtle approach, and who can blame her? She has sweetness as well as cleanness; there are tones of cinnamon, dill, and lemon alongside the mint. Persians put mint in lamb and rhubarb stew; Sicilians add it to tomato salad and tomato sauce or layer it with grilled vegetables bathed in a sweet-sour vinaigrette; Andalusians cook it with oranges and duck. All over the Middle East, whole mint leaves are thrown into salads, mixed into ground lamb, mashed with feta and stirred into pilafs. And what about yogurt, garlic, and mint? That divine trinity is present at almost every Middle Eastern meal I serve. Even the dried stuff is used in the Middle East and, though I find it a bit musty, a swirl of what they call "burned mint" (dried mint fried in butter or oil) looks and tastes good in wintry soups and bowls of yogurt and cucumber.

Fresh, though, mint is never hard to find – it grows so easily that you have trouble finding uses for it. The Moroccans have the perfect solution: mint tea. It's not just that it tastes great, it's that it does great things to your head; clearing, freshening, and soothing all at the same time, leaving you alert but not hyper. No wonder Pliny suggested that students should wear a wreath of mint to "exhilarate their minds". Put a tablespoon of green tea, some sugar and a handful of spearmint leaves in a pot, cover with boiling water and leave to infuse for 5 minutes. Pour the tea from a height to aerate and disperse the perfume and embrace a drink that will make you feel like you've been running in a forest.

Apart from the Persian herb bowl, basil isn't really used in the Middle East. The Greeks regard it as sacred (there you're more likely to see it on the church altar than in the kitchen) and the Moroccans keep it in their gardens to ward off insects (a tribute, I suppose, to its power). But of all these herbs, basil has the greatest capacity to surprise. Tear a leaf in half and smell it. Now taste it. It's full of spices – pepper, cinnamon, and sweet, sweet cloves. It's this sweet pepperiness that makes it a natural in Thai dishes – stir-fried with duck and plums, or shredded into a coconutty stew – and a candidate for experimentation. I've used basil with cilantro and parsley (a taste-bud dazzling combination) in Georgian plum sauce and in lamb or chicken roasts heavy with pomegranates or sour cherries. In fact it's a really good fruit herb. The lemon and basil ice cream in this chapter is quite an obvious pairing, but try basil, too, in ice creams or sorbets made with apples, plums, raspberries, mangoes or pineapples. And put it in the poaching liquid for peaches or nectarines.

As with all these herbs, basil's oils are volatile, so add them to cooked dishes a few minutes before the end. And, just to settle an old culinary conundrum, you should tear basil instead of cutting it if you don't want the edges to go brown. According to culinary scientist Harold McGee, tearing separates the leaves along its cell walls; cutting slices through them. Now you know.

GREEK HERB PILAF WITH SHRIMP AND FETA

Initially I was doubtful about serving shrimp and feta cheese together, but it's a good combination. This dish really smells and tastes like the sea — fishy and salty with a lemony tang — and its fresh greenness is so summery. Don't stint on the herbs or the quality of the olives or olive oil.

serves 4

8oz basmati rice

olive oil

½oz butter

1 onion, finely chopped

1 garlic clove, crushed

9½ oz fresh tomatoes,
   deseeded and
   roughly chopped

a good-sized bunch of
   dill, chopped

a good-sized bunch of flat-leaf
   parsley, chopped

a handful of mint, chopped

salt and pepper

1⅔ cups (14fl oz) fish or
   light chicken stock

¾ lb raw shrimp,
   shelled and de-veined

juice of ½ lemon

2oz black kalamata olives,
   pitted and roughly chopped

extra-virgin olive oil

2¾ oz feta cheese, crumbled

To serve

wedges of lemon

1 Rinse the rice in a sieve until the water runs clear. Leave it to soak for an hour if you can, then rinse again.

2 Heat the butter and 2 tbsp of the oil in a saucepan and cook the onion until it begins to soften. Add the garlic and tomatoes and cook, stirring from time to time, until the onions are translucent and the tomatoes have softened. Stir in the rice and half the herbs, and season. Add the stock and bring it to the boil. Let the liquid boil hard, uncovered, until the rice starts to look "pitted" (little holes appear in the surface of it) and it looks like the liquid has disappeared.

3 Immediately wrap a clean dish towel round the pan lid, being careful to tuck the corners underneath, and cover the pan. Turn the heat down very low and let the rice cook for 20-25 minutes.

4 Just before the rice is ready, quickly sauté the shrimp in a little olive oil over a high heat. Squeeze some lemon juice over them and season with salt and pepper.

5 When the rice is cooked, fork through the olives, the rest of the herbs and lemon juice and a slug of extra-virgin olive oil. Scatter each serving with the crumbled feta and put a mound of shrimp on the top. Drizzle with another drop of extra-virgin olive oil and serve with lemon wedges.

CHILLED AVOCADO AND CILANTRO SOUP

This soup, heady with the fragrance of cilantro, has echoes of Andalucía and North Africa. It's subtle but rich, so serve it in small portions and don't make it too far in advance or the avocado will discolor. If you're making it with chicken stock, don't chill it for too long or the stock will jell, leaving you with a thick gloop rather than a soup.

serves 8

¾ oz butter

2 tbsp olive oil

1 small onion, finely chopped

1 leek, finely sliced

4 cloves garlic, sliced

2 tsp ground cumin

2½ pints (40fl oz)) chicken or
   vegetable stock

12 mint leaves

bunch of cilantro

¼ tsp harissa

salt and pepper

3 medium, ripe avocados

3 plum tomatoes,
   roughly chopped

juice of ½ lime

5 tbsp extra-virgin olive oil

5 tbsp Greek yogurt

To serve

extra-virgin olive oil

fresh cilantro leaves

1 Heat the butter and olive oil together in a saucepan and add the onion, leek, and garlic. Sauté them gently until they begin to soften, then add a splash of water, cover, and let the vegetables sweat for about 15 minutes.

2 Add the cumin, raise the heat a little and cook, stirring, for another minute. Add the stock, mint leaves, a handful of cilantro stalks, *harissa*, salt and pepper. Bring this to the boil and simmer for 15 minutes. Allow the soup to cool.

3 Scoop the flesh out of the avocados, roughly chop them, then add it to the stock with the tomatoes, a couple of handfuls of cilantro leaves and the lime juice. Process in a blender, adding the extra-virgin olive oil. Stir in the Greek yogurt and taste for seasoning. Cover and chill for an hour before serving with a good slug of extra-virgin olive oil and a few cilantro leaves on top.

"Even the worm inside a stone eats herbs."

PERSIAN SAYING

CHERMOULA-MARINATED TUNA WITH POMEGRANATE COUSCOUS

Definitely a dish for cilantro-lovers. Chermoula *is one of the most well-used Moroccan herb and spice blends.* Chermoula *actually means "to tear lightly", but that doesn't stop cooks from making it in the blender. You can use this marinade for chicken or lamb as well as tuna or, made with extra-virgin olive oil, as a sauce or relish.*

serves 4

4 thick tuna loin steaks

salt and pepper

extra-virgin olive oil and lime
   wedges to serve

FOR THE MARINADE

6 tbsp olive oil

3 tsp ground cumin

1½ tsp sweet paprika

¼ tsp ground cinnamon

1 medium red chili,
   deseeded and
   finely chopped

zest and juice of 1 lime

2 garlic cloves, crushed

leaves of a small bunch of
   cilantro and a small bunch
   of flat-leaf parsley, chopped

FOR THE COUSCOUS

7oz couscous

⅔ cup (6fl oz) water

3 tbsp olive oil

2 pomegranates

25g (1oz) pine nuts, toasted

45ml (3 tbsp) each of
   chopped flatleaf parsley
   and mint

lemon juice to taste

1 Mix all the marinade ingredients together in a shallow dish and season with salt and pepper. Turn the tuna steaks over in the marinade to get them well-coated. Refrigerate for about half an hour.

2 Sprinkle the couscous into a shallow dish and add half the water. Let the couscous plump up for about 15 minutes, then fork it through to separate the grains. Repeat with the rest of the water. Stir in the olive oil and some salt and pepper.

3 Halve the pomegranates and, holding each half over a bowl, beat the fruit with a wooden spoon. The seeds should just spill out. Remove any coarse bits of yellow membrane still attached to them.

4 Put the couscous on to steam for about 10 minutes (*see* p119) and, meanwhile, sear the tuna steaks. Heat a griddle until it is smoking hot and then cook the steaks quickly for about 1½ minutes on each side, depending on the thickness. (I serve tuna cooked on the outside and raw as a rare steak on the inside.)

5 Mix the steamed couscous with the pine nuts, pomegranate seeds, herbs, and lemon juice, and check the seasoning. Add a squeeze more lemon if you think the dish needs it. Put a mound of couscous on each plate and serve the tuna steaks on top, drizzled with any remaining marinade and a last slug of extra-virgin olive oil. Serve with wedges of lime.

MACCU WITH FRIED PEPPERS AND MINTED ONIONS

I have a passion for fava beans, both fresh and dried: the former make me think of summer, the latter are definitely autumnal, but both have an essential earthiness. Maccu in Sicily, 'ncapriata in Puglia, and favata in Sardinia, this is a peasant dish, sometimes served as a soup, sometimes as a purée. It's traditionally eaten with cooked wild chicory, but I've also had it with roasted tomatoes, fried peppers and broccoli. The one constant is a generous slick of olive oil. The Egyptians make a minty fava bean purée called besara, and I've stolen the onions and a bit of the seasoning from that dish.

Serves 4 as a main dish, 8 as a side dish

1lb 2oz dried fava beans

1 small onion, finely chopped

1 small carrot, finely chopped

1 celery stick, finely chopped

3 tbsp olive oil

3 garlic cloves, crushed

½ cup (4fl oz) chicken or vegetable stock, or the cooking water from the beans

2½fl oz extra-virgin olive oil

salt and pepper

12 Turkish horn peppers

FOR THE MINTED ONIONS

1½ onions, very finely sliced

2 tbsp olive oil

1 green chili, deseeded and finely chopped

1½ tbsp white-wine vinegar

1 tbsp superfine sugar

a small handful of mint leaves, torn

1 Soak the beans overnight in enough water to cover them. Drain, rinse, and bring them to the boil. Don't salt them, as this will make the beans hard. Simmer for about 1½ hours, until they're tender.

2 Drain the beans, reserving the cooking liquid if you're going to use it. If you haven't got skinned beans, let them cool, then slip the skins off. In 2 tbsp of the olive oil, sauté the onion, carrot, and celery until soft. You'll need to add a little water, stock or bean cooking liquid from time to time, so that everything can cook without drying out. Add the crushed garlic and cook for another minute or so.

3 Put the beans and the sautéed vegetables into a food processor, or mash them if you prefer a coarser purée (and harder work!). Purée while adding the remaining stock or bean cooking liquid and the extra-virgin olive oil. Season with salt and pepper.

4 Put the remaining olive oil into a frying pan and fry the peppers, whole, until they are soft and blistering in patches. Set aside.

5 Using the same pan, cook the sliced onions in the olive oil on a high heat — you want nice brown strings. Add the chili and cook on a lower heat for a further minute. Add the vinegar, sugar, and mint and let the mixture bubble away to allow the vinegar evaporate. Taste and season with salt and pepper.

6 Serve the purée at room temperature, or heat it gently and serve it warm, with the peppers and the onions strewn over the top.

SABZI KHORDAN

The first Persian food I ever tasted was in a prefab in a parking lot in West London. The inside was decorated with tourist posters and the photocopied menu was in Farsi with vague English translations. Alounak, as the "restaurant" was called, was always packed and every meal started, as it does in Iran, with this dish. The idea is to pick at the herbs and roll them up in bits of bread with the cheese, a sliver of onion or a bit of radish. It isn't traditional to serve oil and lemon on the side, but it's a good addition.

serves about 6

good-sized bunches of fresh
    mint, tarragon, cilantro
    and basil
a big bunch of really fresh
    radishes, leaves intact
5½oz feta cheese, broken
    into big chunks
extra-virgin olive oil (optional)
1 red onion
Alounak's Persian flatbread
    (*see* p50)
wedges of fresh lemon to
    serve (optional)

1 Put the herbs, radishes, and feta on a platter. You can leave the herbs in separate bunches or toss them together as you would a salad. Pour a little olive oil, if you want to use it, over the feta.

2 Peel and halve the onion and, cutting from the top to bottom, slice it into half-moon shapes. Add these to the platter in a little pile and serve with warm flatbread, lemon wedges, and a bottle of extra-virgin olive oil.

"They use nothing to whet their Appetites, but some Slices of Lemon, and a few strong Herbs, of which they put a little before every one, with a Radish or two."

SIR JOHN CHARDIN, *TRAVELS IN PERSIA*

ALOUNAK'S PERSIAN FLATBREAD

This bread, known as taftoon *in Iran, is thousands of years old. Iranians cook it by slapping the dough on the burning-hot walls of a wood-fired oven, but you can make a decent version using a hot pizza stone or metal sheets in a fiercely hot domestic oven.*

serves 4

1 tsp dried yeast

½ tsp superfine sugar

1 cup (8fl oz) lukewarm water

9oz bread flour

½ tsp baking powder

1 tsp salt

olive oil

1 Mix the yeast and sugar with a little of the water and leave somewhere warm for 15 minutes, until it froths.

2 Put the rest of the dry ingredients into a bowl and make a well in the center. Pour the yeast into the well and start mixing in the flour from the outside, gradually adding the rest of the warm water as you go. You may not need all the water to bring everything together into a ball, so add a tablespoon at a time towards the end.

3 Knead the dough for 10-15 minutes, until it is smooth and elastic. Put it in a very lightly greased bowl and cover it with a damp dish towel. Leave it somewhere warm to prove for 1½ hours. You can let it rise slowly overnight in the refrigerator if you don't need it until the next day.

4 Set your oven at the highest temperature it can get to (at least 475°F) and put in either metal baking sheets, terracotta tiles or a pita stone to heat up.

5 Take the risen dough out of the bowl and punch it down, lightly kneading it again for a few minutes. Split the dough into four equal pieces and, using a little flour on your work surface and a rolling pin, roll each ball into a circle. With your hands, stretch the dough even further until it is the size of a small dinner plate – it should be thin but not transparent. Put the dough rounds on well-floured baking sheets and cover loosely with plastic wrap. Leave them to prove for about half an hour. Just before you want to cook the bread, take the baking sheets out of the oven and brush with a little olive oil. Put them back into the oven.

6 Prick each round of bread all over with a fork. Wearing a good, thick oven mitt, pick up the bread one piece at a time, take it to the oven and quickly slap it on the heated sheets or pizza stone. It will cook in 3-5 minutes, depending on how hot your oven is, so check after 3 minutes. The bread does not color much, and the dough should be set and chewy, but not hard.

7 Once each piece of bread is cooked, wrap it in a warm dish towel while you cook the others.

TWO SICILIAN PESTOS

I know we've been suffering from pesto overkill lately, but they're always good things to have up your sleeve. The first one here is from the Ristorante da Peppe in Trapani. There they serve it with thin pasta twists called casareccia, *but you can use any pasta shapes. The second pesto is to serve with fish or lamb.*

PESTO ALLA TRAPANESE

4 plum tomatoes, chopped

4 pieces sun-dried tomato, finely chopped

3 garlic cloves, chopped

2¾ oz blanched almonds

a good handful of basil leaves

leaves from 4 sprigs oregano

salt and pepper

2½ fl oz extra-virgin olive oil

2oz pecorino cheese, grated

1 To make this in a food processor simply put all the ingredients, except the olive oil and pecorino, into the bowl. Process it using the pulse button, adding the oil as you do so. Otherwise you can make it in a mortar and pestle. It should be coarser than Pesto Genovese.

2 Stir in the pecorino, check the seasoning, and serve on pasta.

ZOGGHIU

¾ oz each of flat-leaf parsley and mint leaves

2 garlic cloves

extra-virgin olive oil

1½ tsp white-wine vinegar

½ tsp balsamic vinegar

1 tbsp capers, rinsed and chopped

pepper

1 Either tear the herb leaves and then pound them in a mortar and pestle with the garlic, or process them in a food processor using the pulse button, adding the olive oil as you do so.

2 Stir in the vinegars, capers, and pepper. You shouldn't need to add salt because of the saltiness of the capers, but taste to check.

LEMON AND BASIL ICE CREAM

I tasted basil ice cream, made from a recipe in Joyce Molyneaux's Carved Angel Cookery Book, *and loved its sweet, haunting perfumedness. This isn't as subtle, but it's very good. The unsuspecting will be foxed by the flavor.*

serves 4

1¼ cups (10fl oz) milk

30 large basil leaves,
   roughly torn

rind of 1 lemon, cut into
   strips, white pith removed

5½oz superfine sugar

4 egg yolks

juice of 1 lemon

⅝ cup (5fl oz) heavy cream

1 Heat the milk just to boiling point, then take off the heat and add the basil leaves and lemon rind. Let this infuse for about an hour.

2 Beat the sugar and yolks together until pale and fluffy. Strain the milk, pressing the basil and lemon to extract any last bits of flavor. Stir this into the egg and sugar mixture. Make a makeshift bain-marie by putting your bowl into the top of a saucepan of simmering water. Stir the liquid in the bowl constantly until it thickens slightly. If you scrape your finger through the mixture on the back of the spoon and it leaves a path, your custard is ready. Immediately pour it into another bowl and leave to cool.

3 Add the lemon juice to the custard and beat the cream lightly. Add the cream to the custard and freeze in an ice-cream maker, or still-freeze, beating the ice cream three times in a food processor or with an electric beater, during the freezing process.

"Women, vague in the orchard under-shadow, are picking the lemons, lurking as if in the undersea. There are heaps of pale-yellow lemons under the trees. They are pale, primrose-smouldering fires…"

D H LAWRENCE, *SEA AND SARDINIA*

SWEET CLOVES
AND LIQUID GOLD

GARLIC, OLIVES, AND OLIVE OIL

When I was fifteen I had a life-changing cookery lesson. At the kitchen table of a cottage in rural France, with Plastic Bertrand screaming *Ça Plane Pour Moi* out of a tinny radio, I watched a master at work. My penpal Clothilde rubbed a cut clove of garlic around the inside of a china bowl. She then added Dijon mustard, wine vinegar, salt, pepper and a sprinkling of chopped chives. "Always chives?" I asked. "No, sometimes mint, sometimes parsley. *Ça dépend*. But always olive oil," she said as she deftly added a stream of Provençal extra-virgin olive oil, whisking all the time with a fork.

Green leaves of frisée lettuce were tossed into the bowl just before serving and we ate the salad after grilled pork chops marinated in olive oil, garlic, and herbs served with potatoes fried in olive oil and garlic. What a lunch! Garlic had given it a bit of cheeky confidence; olive oil was its soul.

We did have olive oil back home, but it came in a Crosse and Blackwell bottle and was kept for medicinal purposes. Gently warmed, a teaspoonful of this healing syrup would be poured into aching ears. Returning from France, however, I demanded that olive oil be liberated from the medicine cabinet. I wanted it for cooking, marinating, and dressing plain green leaves. There were to be no more vinaigrettes made with sunflower oil and shaken in a jam jar.

It took longer to get into the fruits of the olive tree. Jars of stuffed olives always appeared in the refrigerator before my parents' parties. Little green olives with a flash of red pepper peeping out, they were indelibly marked as grown-ups' food. They whispered of martinis, Manhattan skylines, and dates with men who played Frank Sinatra. But when I tasted them, bitter and briny, they made me shudder.

Later, on holiday in Greece, the olive trees themselves mesmerized me. Grey and gnarled with thousands of silver fishes flickering at their fingertips, they were unknowable; constant yet ever-changing. And their rustle was everywhere. No wonder they confounded painters. Van Gogh told his brother that "The murmur of an olive grove has something very intimate, immensely old. It is too beautiful for me to try to conceive of it or dare to paint it." And Renoir wrote, "Look at the light on the olives. It sparkles like diamonds. It is pink, it is blue, and the sky that plays across them is enough to drive you mad."

When I tried moist purple and black olives on that holiday they tasted salty and sweet, buttery and inky. They still made me shudder – they taste so aggressively of themselves – but now it was a thrill. A hunk of bread, sea salt, extra-virgin olive oil, and a scattering of these shiny bodies became one of my favorite meals. It tasted like an ancient world.

Shimmering among dry rocks and scrubland, olive trees *are* the Mediterranean – a constant reminder of the age of the area – and so sacred in parts of Greece that the olive groves could only be tended by celibate men and virgins. Even today one of the greatest insults a Greek can bestow on someone is to say that he or she is the kind of person who would cut down an olive tree.

But you can only really understand why the olive is such a powerful symbol and so central an ingredient by steeping yourself in its flavors. Think of the simplest dishes – *aglio e olio* (pasta with sautéed garlic and warmed olive oil, and perhaps the addition of chili or parsley), a dish so good you don't even want cheese on it; or the Spanish *pa amb oli* (literally "bread and oil"), where oil is simply poured on toasted bread and seasoned with salt; or *tapenade* – black olives ground with olive oil and garlic to make a paste for bread, a dip for radishes or a kind of relish for grilled lamb and chicken. These are dishes in which food undergoes such minor treatment you could barely call it cooking, in which olives and their oil *are* the dish.

The fruit comes in lots of different shapes, reminiscent of torpedoes, chunky buttons or little beads, and even more flavors. Picked at various stages of maturity, the colors of olives start at unripe sage green and go through pinkish grey, violet, purple, and brown to raven-black. In markets from Marrakesh to Ménerbes huge bowls of olives are perfumed with garlic, thyme or fennel, bathed in olive oil and *harissa*, or flecked with parsley, chili, and pickled lemons. It's easy to prepare your own: buy plain olives from a good delicatessen, wash them if they're in brine, then add extra-virgin olive oil and flavorings. Give them a day and they'll be great; if you can leave them for a week, so much the better. Make slashes through to the stone if you want your aromatics to penetrate further.

Our appreciation of olives and olive oil has come a long way (perhaps too far, I recently thought, watching a chef in a reputed London restaurant pouring extra-virgin over a plate of foie gras). It's fashionable to be fired up over single-estate Tuscans and organic Californians – they're the culinary equivalents of Prada handbags – but try to ignore the snobbery and just taste the stuff. Like wine, the flavor of olive oil depends on the olive variety, soil, climate, and the region in which the fruit is grown as well as on how the oil is processed. The classification of the various grades of oil is strictly monitored. Extra-virgin is the richest oil because it comes from the first pressing of the olives. To classify as extra-virgin, the oil must not be adulterated in any way: the olives mustn't be treated, the oil can be obtained only by pressing, and no other oils can be added. Single-estate extra-virgins, the *grands crus* of the oleaginous world, are, like wine, individual and vary in flavor from year to year. They're expensive and, like all olive oils, they don't keep well (store them in a cool place away from the light), so you can only really have one on the go at a time. But they are so varied that you never tire of using them, and they transform the simplest of dishes: green beans, sliced tomatoes, baked fish, warm pulses, grilled chicken, and fresh broths are all taken to wonderful heights with a distinctive olive oil and a squeeze of lemon. You can choose from the buttery, sweet flavor of an oil from Liguria, the fruitiness of one from Provence, or the grassy bitterness of a bottle of Tuscan.

A blended extra-virgin is good for mustardy vinaigrettes and sauces such as pesto and salsa verde, where you want a good-olive oil taste but know that great subtlety would be lost by other big flavors. A basic olive oil – a refined olive oil mixed with a bit of virgin oil for flavor – is all you need for frying.

You can't really talk about olive oil without, at the same time, thinking of garlic: the faint bass note it gives if rubbed around the salad bowl; the sharpness it provides when grated against oil-drenched toast. Then there are the dishes in which oil and garlic magically combine to produce meals that are almost mystical, their history being so long and their invention so miraculous, such as *aïoli*. It's the garlic mayonnaise the Provençals call *le beurre de Provence* and is central to the feast *le grand aïoli*. Platters of hard-boiled eggs, raw summer vegetables and poached salt cod are served with big bowls of this rich yellow emulsion. Downed with bottles of Provençal rosé, *le grand aïoli* is like eating great punches of sunshine. (And, to be honest, the *aïoli* is wonderful served just with potatoes and none of the extra palaver. Try fries, *aïoli,* and a bottle of Champagne for a fast, glitzy supper).

Then there's *aïoli's* Spanish cousin, the Catalan *all-i-oli* (garlic and oil), a good-with-everything sauce that finds its way into paellas and pasta dishes and is *de rigeur* (or *cosa obligada*?) with chicken, pork, and lamb. In its truest form, *allioli* doesn't contain egg yolks but is an amazing emulsification of crushed garlic and oil. In practice most Catalans do use egg yolk to stabilize the dish, because it is such a fragile concoction, and they also love tinkering with it. You might think that an *allioli* made with the addition of apples, pears or honey sounds revolting, but that is just the sort of delicious culinary surprise a Catalan cook will spring on you.

These mayonnaises use crushed raw garlic, so you get it in its most aggressive form. The more garlic is cut, the more its chemicals are activated and the more pungent the flavor produced. Uncrushed, the flavor is much more subtle. Slice garlic and cook it long and slow in a braise and it will gently infuse the whole dish. Poach garlic in a little stock and cream, purée the cloves and add them back to the reduced cooking liquid and you have a gentle garlicky sauce for rare steak. Roast whole heads of garlic until they're oozing caramel and squeeze the sweet flesh from each clove on bread or grilled meats. New season's garlic, which hasn't yet had a chance to dry to a papery texture and strong flavor, arrives in the shops in June. It's moist and fleshy, tinged with green, and is great roasted and served as a vegetable.

There are only two rules with garlic: never, ever burn it (it turns disgustingly bitter, though slivers of just-browned garlic are delicious) and don't use old stuff; if the head is crumbly or sprouting green shoots, throw it out, because once garlic has seen better days it turns rancid and the smallest piece will ruin your dish.

I'm grateful for that afternoon with Clothilde. It was my first trip abroad and, amid the homesickness and problems with French boys (did they *all* taste of Roquefort when you kissed them?), I experienced a turning point in appreciating the good, but simple, things in life. Clo wouldn't have had much truck with these Tuscans, (well, they're not *French*), but she'd certainly approve of the fact that I have long since abandoned the jam-jar method for making vinaigrette – and that I always go through her soothing ritual of mixing it in the bottom of the salad bowl.

CRAZY WATER

Ah, the title dish. And I must say I initially fell in love with it for its name. It's from the Amalfi coast and nobody really knows why the dish is called "Crazy Water". Some have suggested it alludes to the seawater used by fishermen to cook their catch at sea, others that the "crazy" refers to the heat imparted by the chili. Anyway, you were probably expecting something much more complicated and are now thinking, "So Crazy Water is just poached fish?!" Trust me — you'll love this dish, and guests will rave about it. Get ultra-fresh sea bass, offer excellent extra-virgin olive oil and revel in luxurious simplicity. I particularly like bass, but you can use other fish for your pesce all'acqua pazza, *too.*

serves 4

3lb 5oz sea bass, or 4 small
  sea bass, gutted and scaled
really good extra-virgin olive oil
  and wedges of lemon,
  for serving

FOR THE BROTH

1 medium bunch
  flat-leaf parsley
8 large plum tomatoes,
  deseeded and chopped
2 small red chilies (not bird's
  eye – they're too hot),
  deseeded and finely chopped
3 garlic cloves, finely chopped
7fl oz white wine
1¼ cup (10fl oz) fish stock
  or water
4 sprigs oregano, or about
  1 tbsp dried
  oregano, crumbled
3½fl oz extra-virgin olive oil
salt and pepper

1 To make the broth, cut the stalks off the parsley and tie about half a dozen of them together with a piece of string. Put the leaves to one side. Mix all the ingredients for the broth, excluding the parsley leaves but including the bundle of stalks, in the bottom of a pan large enough to hold the fish. Bring it up to the boil, then turn down to a simmer and cook for 15 minutes.

2 Wash the fish well and lower it into the pan of broth. Cover and simmer gently for about 30 minutes for a large fish, 15 for small ones. Do check from time to time to see how it's doing. You need to look at the flesh nearest the bone: if it's white, the fish is cooked; if it's translucent, it needs more time.

3 Remove the fish, then cover it and keep it warm while you finish off the broth. Whip out the parsley stalks, bring the broth up to the boil and let it reduce by about a quarter. Roughly chop the parsley leaves and, keeping a handful aside for garnish, throw them into the pan and let it simmer for another 3 or 4 minutes while you deal with the fish.

4 If you've cooked one large fish, you can serve it whole on a platter, with the broth in a tureen on the side. Or you can serve the broth in individual broad soup plates, with the flesh from a large fish or whole small fish on top. However you present it, douse liberally with really good extra-virgin olive oil – offering more on the side – and sprinkle a few parsley leaves on top. Serve with lemon wedges and either new potatoes or bread.

Il pesce vive nell'acqu, e deve affogare nel vino.

"Since fish thrives in water, it must be drowned in wine."

ITALIAN SAYING

SEARED TUNA WITH POTATO SKORDALIA AND CAPER VINAIGRETTE

Skordalia is a Greek sauce made with crushed garlic and either potato or breadcrumbs, or a bit of both, beaten with olive oil — a kind of Greek aïoli. It's usually served as a sauce for raw vegetables or salt-cod fritters, but this version gives you a garlicky "mash" rather than a dip.

serves 4

4 thick tuna loin steaks

olive oil

salt and pepper

balsamic vinegar

flat-leaf parsley to serve

FOR THE VEGETABLES

10 plum tomatoes

2 tbsp olive oil

1 tbsp balsamic vinegar

1 tsp superfine sugar

2 eggplants

1 tsp dried Greek oregano
(*rigani*)

FOR THE DRESSING

4 tbsp extra-virgin olive oil

2 tbsp balsamic vinegar

2 tbsp capers, rinsed

FOR THE SKORDALIA

1lb potatoes, peeled

3 garlic cloves, crushed

1½ tbsp white-wine vinegar

¾ cup (6fl oz) extra-virgin
   olive oil

2 tbsp heavy cream

1 Cut each tomato in half lengthwise and put them into a small roasting pan. Add half of the olive oil and balsamic vinegar and turn the tomatoes over in this to make sure they get coated, finishing with them cut-side-up. Sprinkle with the sugar and some salt and pepper. Roast in an oven preheated to 400°F while you prepare the eggplants.

2 Cut each eggplant into slices about a half-inch thick, then quarter each slice. Stir these chunks around in a bowl with the rest of the oil and vinegar and, after the tomatoes have roasted for 20 minutes, add the eggplant, sprinkle with oregano, and cook for another 20 minutes. When the vegetables are done you can let them sit, covered in foil, for an hour or so, as they are fine served tepid.

3 Make the dressing by mixing the ingredients together with a little salt and pepper.

4 For the *skordalia*, cook the potatoes in boiling water until tender. Drain, mash roughly, and then push them through a potato ricer or sieve. Put the mash back in the saucepan and place over a very low heat. Add the garlic and vinegar and season with salt and pepper. Pour in the olive oil very gradually, beating as you go, until it's amalgamated. Add the cream and check the seasoning. Take the pan off the heat, but cover it to keep the *skordalia* warm.

5 Just before you want to serve, brush each piece of tuna with oil, and season. Heat a griddle until it is very hot. Cook the fish for about 1½ minutes on each side — this will give you tuna which is like rare steak; brown on the outside, pink and melting on the inside. Cook it for longer if you prefer to, but be careful that it doesn't get dry. In the final seconds, throw on a good slosh of balsamic vinegar and let it bubble away, turning the tuna over once in the vinegar. It gives a wonderful glaze.

6 Put some skordalia on each plate with a mound of roast vegetables on top and then your tuna. Drizzle the dressing round the outside of the dish and finish with a sprig of flat-leaf parsley.

FIDEUA WITH ALLIOLI

God, this is a good dish! It was first cooked for me by a guy called Dave Hayward (a man so in love with all things Spanish that he even has the snails for his paellas sent from Spain… Enough said.) Fideuá is a kind of pasta paella. In Spain they use tiny noodles, but they're pretty hard to get hold of so I use slim, twisted pasta shapes called casareccia, *which I prefer anyway. Other people use short bits of broken spaghetti. The first time you make this dish, add your stock gradually so you don't end up with cooked pasta swimming in liquid; the amount of stock you need will depend on the cooking time of the pasta you use. Just make sure you use durum wheat — not egg — pasta, and don't even be tempted to stir!*

serves 4

1¾ lb raw shrimp, peeled
   and de-veined

olive oil

1 onion, finely chopped

5½ oz tomatoes,
   roughly chopped

1 tsp *pimentón de la Vera*
   (sweet smoked
   Spanish paprika)

about 4¼ cups (34 fl oz) fish
   stock or light chicken stock

12oz noodles, *casareccia,* or
   other small pasta

salt and pepper

a small handful of flat-leaf
   parsley, roughly chopped

wedges of lemon

FOR THE ALLIOLI

2 garlic cloves

sea salt

2 egg yolks

1¼ cups (10fl oz) mild
   extra-virgin olive oil

ground white pepper

lemon juice

white-wine vinegar

1 Heat a little oil in a sauté pan and quickly cook the shrimp until they turn pink. Remove them and set aside.

2 In the same pan cook the onion, adding another 1 tbsp olive oil if you need to, until soft and just turning golden. Add the tomatoes and the *pimentón*, and stir everything together. Cook the mixture for about 15 minutes, until it's soft and thick. Pour on the stock and bring to the boil. Add the pasta and season. Don't cover the pan, but just leave it to cook, without stirring, for about 15 minutes, or until the pasta is tender. The stock should have been absorbed.

3 Make the *allioli* while the pasta is cooking. Crush the garlic with a little salt in a large mortar or bowl. Stir in the egg yolks. Add the oil drop by drop, beating with a wooden spoon or hand mixer as you do so. Only add more oil once the previous lot has been incorporated and the mixture has thickened. If your mixture does split and you end up with curdled egg swimming in oil, you just need to start again with another egg yolk. Add the curdled mixture to the new yolk while beating, just as before, but patiently this time!

4 When you've added all the oil, season with more salt, some pepper, and lemon juice and wine vinegar to taste. It's better for you to taste as you go along than for me to be specific. Cover and put the *allioli* in the fridge until you need it; I never keep it for more than a day.

5 Put the shrimp back in the pan, add the parsley and cook until the fish is heated through. Stir in a couple of tablespoons of *allioli* and serve with the rest of the *allioli* and wedges of lemon on the side.

CATALAN BLACK RICE WITH ALLIOLI

I first had arroz negro *in a village near Barcelona about eighteen years ago. It was a bit of a shock — jet-black rice which left my teeth and lips alarmingly inky. Little did I realize how fashionable black rice would become. Mostly, though, it's black risotto that has done the rounds rather than the Spanish version. Anyway, eaten with* allioli *(it might seem like overkill but I, like the Catalans, think* allioli *enhances most things) and sweet scallops, this dish is above the vagaries of fashion. Another plus is that* arroz negro, *made with Spanish calasparra rice (and you have to use that) must not be stirred. That's definitely one up on Risotto Nero. Ask the guy at the fish counter to get sachets of squid ink for you.*

serves 4

1lb 5oz squid, cleaned

4 tbsp olive oil

1 onion, finely chopped

3 plum tomatoes, roughly
    chopped

1 garlic clove, finely
    chopped

10½oz Spanish Calasparra rice

6 sachets squid ink

5 cups (about 40fl oz) hot
    fish stock

salt and pepper

a small bunch of flat-leaf
    parsley

juice of ½ lemon

allioli to serve (*see* p61)

FOR THE SCALLOPS

olive oil

8 scallops, cleaned, roe intact

1 lemon, halved

1 Cut the squid bodies into quarter-inch slices. Cut the tentacles in half if they are long. Heat 2 tbsp of the olive oil in a heavy-bottomed frying pan or paella pan. Once it's hot, quickly sauté the squid for about 30 seconds then lift it out and set aside. Add the rest of the oil and gently sauté the onion until soft and translucent — don't let it color. Stir in the tomatoes and the garlic and cook for another couple of minutes over a medium heat, then turn the heat down low and let the vegetables cook until very soft and quite thick — it will take about 15 minutes. Add another drop of olive oil if you need it.

2 Tip in the rice and stir it into the tomatoes. Squeeze the ink into the stock and add that, too. Season lightly — by the time the stock's absorbed it will make the dish quite salty. Reserve a few of the parsley leaves, then roughly chop the rest and add to the pan as well. Stir briefly just to mix everything together. Bring the liquid up to the boil, then turn it down to a simmer and let the rice cook for 20-25 minutes, by which time the stock should have been absorbed. Keep an eye on it and add a little water if you think the stock has been absorbed too quickly and the rice is in danger of boiling dry. You must try not to stir the mixture, though you can have a careful peek to check what's going on at the bottom of the pan.

3 Add the squid to the rice for the last 5 minutes of the cooking time. Season with the lemon juice, salt, and pepper, and taste. Cover the pan and let it sit for another 5 minutes to rest before serving.

4 Heat a little oil in a frying pan and, when it's very hot, quickly sauté the scallops for about 30 seconds on each side. Sprinkle some salt and pepper on them and a squeeze of lemon juice.

5 Serve the rice in flat soup plates with a dollop of the *allioli*, a couple of scallops per person and a few of the reserved parsley leaves. Put the rest of the *allioli* in a bowl on the table — some people can't get enough of it.

"*Frédéric Mistral, to the very best of my knowledge the only poet ever to have been named after a minor European wind, wrote the 'Aïoli epitomizes the heat, the power, and the joy of the Provençal sun, but it has another virtue — it drives away flies'.*"

JOHN LANCHESTER, *THE DEBT TO PLEASURE*

SICILIAN TUNA IN STEMPERATA SAUCE

Sicily is tuna heaven. The fish is served in hundreds of different ways — in countless tomato sauces, with almonds, with oranges, with vinegar and onions, raw, marinated, with pasta and without. Many of the dishes, like this one, are sweet and sour, showing the island's Arab legacy. This sauce is a cinch to make, can be prepared in advance, and tastes great.

serves 4

4 thick tuna loin steaks

olive oil

salt and pepper

balsamic vinegar

extra-virgin olive oil to serve

FOR THE SAUCE

4 celery sticks, plus the
    leaves, finely chopped

½ red onion, finely chopped

2 tbsp olive oil

3 garlic cloves, minced

5½oz green olives, pitted,
    some halved, some
    roughly chopped

6oz capers, rinsed

2¾oz raisins, plumped up in a
    little hot water, and drained

3 tbsp white-wine vinegar

1 tbsp fresh oregano,
    finely chopped

freshly ground black pepper

1 For the sauce, sauté the celery and onion in the olive oil until soft and just beginning to turn golden. Add the garlic, olives, capers, and raisins and cook for another couple of minutes. Add the vinegar, oregano, and some freshly ground black pepper, and cook until the vinegar has evaporated. Set aside. You can either serve this sauce at room temperature, or quickly reheat it while the tuna is cooking.

2 When you want to serve, rub olive oil, salt, and pepper on each side of the fish steaks and heat a ridged griddle until very hot. Cook the tuna for 1-1½ minutes on each side. This will give you tuna which is like a rare steak – charred on the outside, pink and melting on the inside. In the final few seconds, throw on a slosh of balsamic vinegar and let it bubble away, turning the tuna over once in the vinegar once. It gives a wonderful glaze.

3 Serve the tuna immediately with the *stemperata* sauce and a drizzle of extra-virgin olive oil.

> *"Olive groves,*
>
> *may God bestow*
>
> *January showers*
>
> *to make you grow*
>
> *and in August groundwater below;*
>
> *winds in spring*
>
> *for your clustered bloom*
>
> *and autumn rains*
>
> *for your purple fruit."*
>
> ANTONIO MACHADO, "THE OLIVE TREES",
> *SELECTED POEMS*

QUAIL EGGS WITH RADISHES, ANCHOVY MAYO, AND TUNA TAPENADE

This makes the most beautiful and abundant looking starter, stylish but far from flamboyant. I've been making tapenade — *a kind of Provençal gentleman's relish — with tuna as well as the requisite capers, anchovies, and olives for years. The Provençaux argue about whether this is correct, but it tastes good so who cares? It's a treat to have a bowl of it in the fridge for snacking on.*

Serves 6 as a starter

24 quail eggs

a bunch of French breakfast
   radishes, with leaves

FOR THE MAYO

2 egg yolks

½ tsp Dijon mustard

1 tbsp white-wine vinegar

150ml (5fl oz) mild extra-virgin
   olive oil

⅝ cup (5fl oz) sunflower oil

1½ tbsp capers, rinsed

2 tbsp flat-leaf
   parsley, chopped

1oz anchovy, chopped

salt and white pepper

lemon juice, to taste

FOR THE TAPENADE

1 x 7oz can tuna in olive
oil, drained

2 x 2oz cans anchovies in
   olive oil

5½ oz (drained weight)
   black olives, pitted

juice of ½ lemon

2 garlic cloves, crushed

¼ cup (2fl oz) extra-virgin
   olive oil

1 tbsp brandy

leaves of 2 sprigs of thyme

2 tbsp chopped fresh parsley

1 For the mayo, mix the egg yolks with the Dijon mustard and half of the vinegar in the bottom of a bowl. Beating all the time with a wooden spoon, whisk or hand beater, start adding the oils very slowly, drop by drop. Wait until each drop of oil is well-amalgamated and the mixture has thickened before adding the next bit.

2 When you have a thick purée, and have incorporated all the oils, add the rest of the wine vinegar plus the capers, parsley, and anchovies. Mix this all together and add salt, pepper, and lemon juice to taste. Cover and keep in the refrigerator.

3 To make the tapenade, simply put all the ingredients in the food processor and blend. Use the pulse button if you want a coarse purée.

4 Bring a pan of water to the boil and then cook the eggs for 4 minutes; they should be just hard-boiled. When they're cool enough to handle, half-peel ten of the eggs (it just looks nice) and put all the eggs on a plate with the radishes.

5 Serve the *tapenade* and mayo in separate bowls alongside the eggs and radishes and provide unsalted butter, sea salt, and French bread.

SALT-BAKED POTATOES WITH CREME FRAICHE AND NEW SEASON'S GARLIC

To make this side dish into a light main course, double the quantity and serve with fresh goat cheese and a green salad.

Serves 4 as an appetizer or side dish

9½oz coarse sea salt

about 6 sprigs thyme

1½lb new potatoes, scrubbed

8 heads new season's garlic

olive oil

salt and pepper

To serve

1 x 7fl oz pot crème fraîche
   or sour cream

1 Sprinkle the salt and thyme into a small ovenproof pot or roasting pan. Half-bury the potatoes in the salt and cover very tightly with foil. Bake in an oven preheated to 325°F for 1½ hours.

2 Put the garlic in another small roasting pan, drizzle on some olive oil and season. Pour a little cold water into the bottom of the pan and roast the garlic for about 50 minutes, adding more water every so often when the pan gets dry. The garlic should be completely soft with slightly caramelized skin.

3 Serve the heads of garlic whole, along with the potatoes, and the crème fraîche on the side. Everyone can slit their potatoes, daub them with cream, and eat them along with the soft garlic cloves squeezed out of their skins.

MOUTARDE DE PROVENCE

This is a fabulous sauce, based on a recipe in Patience Gray's idiosyncratic book about eating and cooking around the Mediterranean, Honey from a Weed. *This sauce is good with steak, lamb, chicken or meaty fish or spread on hot toast.*

Serves 6

5 heads garlic

olive oil

6 anchovy filets, soaked in a
   little milk and drained

freshly ground black pepper

meat or chicken juices

½ tsp balsamic
   vinegar (optional)

1 Remove the outer papery covering from the garlic, but don't separate or peel the cloves. Put them in a small ovenproof dish and drizzle a bit of olive oil over each bulb. Pour a little water around them – only about a quarter of a wine glass – so that some steam can be created. Put them in an oven preheated to 350°F and cook for 40-50 minutes, until they are soft and slightly colored. You will need to add a little water every so often.

2 Pound the anchovies and a little pepper in a mortar, or mash them in a bowl. Cut into the heads of garlic and squeeze the flesh from each clove. Add this to the anchovies and crush everything together. If this is to serve with lamb or chicken, incorporate some meat juices, too. I also like a little balsamic vinegar in it, but taste the mixture first – you may be happy without it.

CATALAN CHICKEN WITH QUINCE ALLIOLI

Here is Catalan allioli *again, but with a twist. You might think that the idea of garlic and oil with sweet things is disgusting, but this is delicious and unexpected. You can also make it with apples or pears, and try serving it with lamb or pork as well as chicken. I make the* allioli *by hand in a big pestle and mortar, partly because it becomes frothy and aerated in a food processor, but also because it's really satisfying to feel the changing texture as the oil is added.*

serves 4-6

1 x 3¾lb roasting chicken
olive oil and sea salt

FOR THE STUFFING

½ medium onion,
    finely chopped
2½ oz pancetta, chopped
1 tbsp olive oil
1oz pine nuts
10½oz pork, ground
2¾oz breadcrumbs
1 small egg, beaten
leaves from 4 sprigs thyme
2 tbsp chopped
    flat-leaf parsley
nutmeg, freshly grated
salt and pepper

FOR THE *ALLIOLI*

1 large quince, peeled, cored
    and cut into chunks
2 garlic cloves
½ tsp sea salt
2½fl oz mild extra-virgin
    olive oil
a good squeeze of lemon juice
1 tsp white-wine vinegar
1 tbsp clear honey

1 First make the stuffing. Sauté the onion and pancetta in the olive oil until golden. Tip this into a medium bowl and fry the pine nuts in the same pan until they've started to brown a little. Add them to the bowl, along with the minced pork, breadcrumbs, beaten egg, thyme, parsley, and seasonings. Mix everything well.

2 Rinse the chicken inside and out, pat dry with paper towels, and stuff. Place in a roasting pan, pour a little olive oil over the top, sprinkle with sea salt, and roast in an oven preheated to 350°F for about 1½ hours.

3 To make the *allioli*, put the quince chunks in a pan and cover with a little water. Cook until tender; this could take as long as 30 minutes. Drain. Cut the garlic cloves in half and remove any bitter green inner shoot. Pulverize the garlic with salt in a mortar, then add the quince and crush it to a purée. Slowly add the olive oil, a drop at a time, beating as you go, until the oil amalgamates and you have a thick purée. Add the lemon juice, vinegar, and honey and refrigerate the *allioli* until you need it.

4 Carve the chicken, and hand the *allioli* around in a bowl so that people can help themselves.

SPAGHETTI WITH MOLLICA AND OLIO SANTO

Holy oil, or olio santo, *is Sicilian hot oil. With a bottle of this in your cupboard, you will always be able to have a delicious, impromptu meal instead of shelling out for a delivery. You can make a job lot of* mollica *(that's Sicilian for fried breadcrumbs), and keep it in an airtight container for just these occasions. Drizzle the oil over pizza, fish or grilled chicken, too.*

serves 4-6

1lb spaghetti

salt and black pepper

3½oz slightly stale country
    bread, without the crusts

olive oil

2oz pine nuts

5 garlic cloves, sliced

a large bunch of parsley, finely
    chopped

a good squeeze of lemon juice

FOR THE HOLY OIL

1 bottle extra-virgin olive oil

3 long red chilies

3 bird's eye chilies

3 bay leaves

1 tbsp black
    peppercorns, crushed

1 To make the *olio santo*, pour a little of the extra-virgin olive oil out of the bottle and keep it for something else – you just need to make some room for the herbs and spices. Make sure all your chilies are fresh; any signs of decay and you'll end up with a bottle of rancid oil. Cut two of the long chilies and one of the small ones into rounds. Add all the chilies to the bottle of oil with the bay leaves and pepper. Leave aside for a couple of weeks, somewhere dark, and shake from time to time. It will keep as long as the oil itself.

2 Cook the spaghetti in plenty of boiling, salted water. To make the *mollica*, grate or process the bread into crumbs. Heat about 4 tbsp of olive oil in a pan and fry the crumbs for 3 minutes, until golden, stirring from time to time. Put them in a bowl and set them aside.

3 Heat 2 tbsp of the holy oil and fry the pine nuts in this, adding the garlic just as the nuts are beginning to color. Be careful not to burn the garlic; just cook it until golden.

4 Drain the spaghetti and put it back into the saucepan with about 6-8 tbsp of the holy oil. Heat gently and add salt and pepper, parsley, the garlic, and nuts, and lemon juice to taste.

5 Toss the pasta in a large warmed bowl, or on individual plates, with the *mollica* sprinkled on top, and serve with extra holy oil on the side.

"The whole Mediterranean ... all of it seems to rise in the sour, pungent taste of these black olives between the teeth. A taste older than meat, older than wine. A taste as old as cold water."

LAWRENCE DURRELL, *PROSPERO'S CELL*

OLIVE OIL AND MOSCATO CAKE WITH BAKED APRICOTS

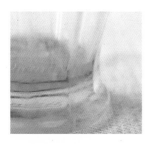

This cake, adapted from a recipe in the Chez Panisse Menu Cookbook *by Alice Waters, is a revelation: light and fragrant but rich at the same time. It's also good served with plain sliced peaches or nectarines and a glass of chilled Moscato.*

Uncooked, most apricots disappoint — they often have woolly flesh and none of the perfume their appearance seems to promise — but cooking brings out their honeyed tartness. Cooked this way, they make a great dessert just by themselves with cream — but do use decent vanilla.

Serves 8

5 eggs

3½oz superfine sugar

5 tbsp extra-virgin olive oil

⅝ cup (5fl oz) Moscato, or
    other dessert wine

3½oz all-purpose flour, sifted

½ tsp salt

2 egg whites

½ tsp cream of tartar

confectioner's sugar for sifting

FOR THE APRICOTS

20 large apricots

1⅝ cups (13fl oz) white wine

1 vanilla pod, or 1½ tsp
    good vanilla extract

6oz superfine sugar

1 Butter an eight-inch springform cake pan and line the base with baking parchment. Separate the eggs and beat the yolks together with half the sugar until pale and thick. Add the olive oil and the Moscato. Fold in the flour and salt.

2 Beat the rest of the sugar with all the egg whites and the cream of tartar until they hold medium peaks. Fold into the egg and flour mixture and pour into the cake pan. Bake in an oven preheated to 350°F for 20 minutes, then turn down to 300°F and bake for another 30 minutes. Turn off the oven, cover the cake with a circle of buttered paper, and leave it in the oven for a further 10 minutes. Remove and let the cake cool in its pan.

3 Halve the apricots and remove the stone. Put them in a single layer, skin-side up, in overlapping circles, in an ovenproof dish. Pour on the wine. Slit the vanilla pod along its length, scrape out the seeds and add these to the wine, along with the pod.

4 Spoon the sugar over the top and bake in an oven preheated to 350°F for 20 minutes. The apricots should be soft and slightly caramelized on top.

5 Sift some confectioner's sugar over the cake and serve with the apricots, either chilled or at room temperature, with cream or mascarpone on the side.

THE SWEET
AND THE SOUR

HONEY AND VINEGAR

Honey has something of a split personality, or maybe just a complex one. On the one hand it's cute, domestic, and dependable – a barrel-shaped jar of sunshine sitting on your breakfast table. You've been aware of honey since you were little when, after milk, it was one of the first foods you learned about. Labored over by the coolest dressers in the insect world, it was eaten by Pooh, Yogi, and any other bear you care to mention. Harmless, sweet honey. Good old hard-working bees. Yet on the other hand honey is more than just something sweet to spread on toast. Honey is sustaining and seems almost miraculous. It is thought of as mystical, a gift from the gods, with an ambrosial flavor beyond the imagination. God's "manna from heaven" is described in the Bible as tasting "like wafers made with honey". And when we use the word "honeyed" we don't just mean sweet; we also mean soft, warm, unctuous and even sexy. Listening to Van Morrison growling "She's as sweet as Tupelo honey" you don't get the impression he means "she's" just a nice girl!

Part of honey's magic is the very thing we found enchanting about it when we were children: how it's made. For a start, humans aren't in charge of it – insects are. Teams of bees diligently tend complex structures, building and repairing waxen cells, collecting nectar, looking after the queen bee and her offspring. The bees even run their own cooling system, flapping their wings to create a draught which thickens the honey by driving off moisture. And all this activity doesn't just make honey, it pollinates plants. What a great design! What a harmonious whole! A natural phenomenon which works for everyone.

Not everything about honey is absolutely pure. Commercial jars are usually made from blended honeys, which have been heated so that they won't crystallize, thus destroying some of the oils that give honey its flavor. Most honeys, the cheap and boutique, are filtered to remove wax and the odd bee's leg, but that's about it. No additives or preservatives are required – your pot of nectar transformed by nothing more than bees' saliva, is one of the most unadulterated foods you can get.

The taste of honey is as mysterious as its manufacture – or at least as hard to define. It isn't just sweet; it encompasses a whole range of flavors, and it's difficult to describe them without recourse to foods that are also described as "honeyed": quinces, mangoes, lychee nuts, and wines such as Sauternes and Riesling. I always liked honey as a child, but it wasn't until my sister brought a big waxen tub of it home from a skiing holiday that I realized there is more to honey than meets the eye. It was a floral alpine honey, a veritable bucketful of it: thick-set, creamy-colored, and light-years away from the jar of amber stuff that sat in the cupboard alongside the marmalade. Years later I made a pilgrimage to a Parisian honey shop I'd read about and became a born-again honey-lover. The Maison de Miel is a quintessentially French creation, a blend of high-tech and tradition. The lady behind the counter wears a white lab coat, just in case you aren't going to take your honeys seriously, but the shelves behind her are stacked with golden-filled jars bearing the old-fashioned *Maison de Miel* label. Madame, in delightful Parisian singsong, implores you to try whatever you fancy.

Most of the honeys in Maison de Miel are what enthusiasts call "monoflorals", made with nectar from single flower varieties. There's delicately perfumed orange blossom, pungent and macho chestnut, and menthol-scented eucalyptus. There are regional differences, too: the wild flowers of the French Jura produce different honeys from the wild flowers of Tuscany. If you're buying without tasting, generally the darker the honey, the stronger the taste. I've tried lots of flavors over the years and my favorite has to be lavender. It simply tastes of its smell, perfectly encapsulating a hot afternoon in Provence. It's a minor miracle that something so evanescent can be captured in a jar.

Before the discovery of sugar cane and beets, the only sweetener available was honey, and the Middle East has clung to it as a basic ingredient – crushed nuts are bound with spoonfuls of thick honey and wrapped in parchment-like sheets of pastry; honey syrups are poured over still-warm cakes and into the crevices of flaky filo; and feta-stuffed parcels are drizzled with honey. But you can turn out easier, more modern desserts that have the same eastern accent. Heat honey gently and add lime or orange juice, then perfume it with orange-flower water, crushed cardamoms, saffron or cinnamon to make a syrup for pouring on ice cream, rice puddings, pannacotta, poached apples, mangoes, peaches or melon. Or just pour orange-blossom honey over drained yogurt, sprinkle with pistachios, and serve with sliced oranges. Drizzle a puddle of honey beside a hunk of cheese – ewes milk cheeses such as Spanish *manchego* and Italian *pecorino* make good partners. Spoon chestnut honey onto baked pears and sprinkle with toasted walnuts and Gorgonzola; or serve a chunk of comb honey with a wedge of *dolcelatte*, a bowl of mascarpone, and a pile of ripe white peaches – simple, natural, fulsome and magical.

Fruity Moroccan *tajines* are unthinkable without honey – stirring streams of mahogany sweetness into a dark, glossy potful of lamb, raisins, and almonds is one of the more sensuous pleasures in cooking – and simpler Meditteranean dishes can be made by using it in a marinade. Roast a leg of lamb in honey, crushed coriander, and chili; bake chicken joints in honey, cumin, lemon, olive oil and garlic; grill duck breasts slathered with honey, sherry vinegar, and ginger. They all cook to a burnished sheen, like polished chestnuts, and have the bittersweet taste of caramelized sugar and spice. One word of advice, though: if you're going to subject your honey to direct heat, use a blended honey, since broiling will spoil the nuances of a complex or delicate one. For strong dishes such as *tajines*, use pungent ones which can stand up to meaty ingredients and long, slow cooking. Only use delicate monoflorals in dishes that allow their taste to come through, or for more unadulterated pleasures. Spread monoflorals on toast, drizzle them over yogurts, mix them with cream to fill a cake or to serve with figs, make them into ice cream for which you only heat the honey enough to liquify it, or use them for mousses.

Honey and vinegar, so opposed in flavor, have an affinity precisely because they are poles apart. And their combined charms are not limited to a "number 37" from your local Chinese take-out. I love using them together in vinaigrettes, especially for dishes that can meet the flavors head-on, such as salads of bitter leaves, wild and brown rice, and quartered figs with strong cheeses. I also like them together in marinades; try honey, balsamic vinegar, and lavender for poussins. And use them to make quick, fruity sweet-and-sour sauces – deglaze a pan in which you've cooked duck with a little balsamic, throw in a handful of blueberries and a bit of strong chicken stock, cook until the berries are softening and the stock has reduced, add a drop of honey, a knob of unsalted butter, and a little pepper, and there you have it.

Cooked, balsamic vinegar adds a wonderful grapy, burnt-sugaryness to food. I never roast tomatoes without sprinkling balsamic on top, and it's good on other Mediterranean vegetables, as well as on mushrooms, onions, and potatoes. It's also great with meat: marinate a leg of lamb in a little balsamic, olive oil, rosemary, and garlic before roasting and you'll see. You can't just hold the bottle upside-down and pour, mind you; you have to use balsamic carefully, adding it in those maddeningly imprecise quantities, a drizzle, a *soupçon* or a slug, and getting to know, in time, how much is right for certain foods.

Of course, you shouldn't be using your $30 bottle of *aceto balsamico tradizionale* for cooking. There are two types of balsamic vinegar, and the word *tradizionale* makes all the difference. All balsamics are made from reduced grape must rather than wine, but the characteristic caramelized flavor is achieved in the cheaper bottles by adding sugar. Cheaper balsamic may be aged in barrels in the same way as the expensive type, but for a much shorter period of time, and the label will simply say *aceto balsamico*.

The *tradizionale* must be allowed to speak for itself. Add splashes of it to raw vine tomatoes, warm beans, and perfectly cooked fish. Its sharp sweetness is also great with slices of fatty prosciutto and certain fruits. In Italy I was once served a heavenly dessert of raspberries, sugar, and a spoonful of mascarpone streaked with a flash of aged balsamic – a fantastically chic-but-no-effort dessert if you're willing to shell out on the vinegar. And a drop of balsamic in homemade strawberry ice cream gives an even more intensely strawberry result.

Sherry vinegar, made from fermented sherry, looks just like balsamic vinegar: slightly syrupy and a deep, dark brown (the color of Latin eyes). But its nutty woodiness lets you know immediately that it's made from sherry and it doesn't have the sweet caramel tones of balsamic vinegar. You have to use sherry vinegar even more carefully or it will drown every other flavor in a dish. Some producers are starting to bottle their vinegar with a dash of sherry added to it, something you could try yourself in a vinaigrette; it just rounds out the flavor. But sherry vinegar's power is also its strength. It tastes supremely of Spain. Just one splash has the blur of red flamenco dresses flashing before your eyes.

Under the hot sun of the Middle East, vinegar is loved for its mouth-puckering flavor and has always been essential as a preservative. Iranians look forward to the first meals of spring and their chance to dip fresh young lettuce leaves into a sweet, vinegary syrup. And pickles are served all over the Middle East as part of *mezze*. Jars of pickles, stuffed with a multitude of colors, from the vibrant crimson of beetroot to the cool sage-green of beans, line the shelves of kitchens and groceries. Vinegar soaks rounds of carrot, shreds of red cabbage and chunks of turnip. Even quinces, cloves of garlic, walnut-stuffed baby eggplants, and black and green grapes get the pickling treatment, and they all go well with the earthy and the sweet flavors which dominate Middle Eastern meals.

AJO BLANCO

This, a kind of white gazpacho, is an amazing dish. The worst cooks can't mess it up, you can make it in the last ten minutes before guests arrive, and the unpromising ingredients of old bread, almonds, garlic, water, and oil are whipped into something eminently appetizing. Needless to say, neither your almonds nor your garlic should be old; in fact, plenty of purists would pound freshly shelled almonds in a mortar and pestle — or so they tell me. Your stale bread should have been good in the first place and your oil should be the best. Serve ajo blanco *well-chilled in very small portions — it's pretty rich.*

serves 4-6

6oz day-old white country
    bread, crusts removed

a little milk

7oz blanched almonds

3 garlic cloves

¾ cup (6fl oz) extra-virgin
    olive oil

1¾ cups (14fl oz) very cold
    water

2 tbsp sherry vinegar

salt and pepper

about 32 seedless white
    grapes, with more available

1 Soak the bread in enough milk to moisten it. Leave for a couple of hours, then squeeze the milk out.

2 Put the bread into a food processor with the almonds and the garlic. With the motor running, add the oil gradually, followed by the water. Season with the sherry vinegar, salt, and pepper. Stir, then taste to check whether you would like any more water or seasoning.

3 Peel the grapes — come on, think of it as therapeutic. Whether you serve the soup in individual bowls or take it to the table in a tureen, scatter the peeled grapes on top and drizzle with more extra-virgin olive oil. I love the grapes with it, so I always serve more on the side, though I never get round to peeling the extra ones…

"Delicate almond; promise of wonders; little kernel; tiny springtime that sleeps as it waits."

ANDRE GIDE, *FRUITS OF THE EARTH*

ARAB-ANDALUSIAN MONKFISH WITH SAFFRON, HONEY, AND VINEGAR

Sweet and sour and imbued with saffron, this is a real Arab-Andalusian dish. I really like it with couscous into which I've stirred some shreds of preserved lemon.

serves 4

olive oil

salt and pepper

4 small monkfish tails

1 large onion, finely sliced

½ tsp ground cinnamon

1 medium red chili, deseeded
    and finely chopped

¾ cup (6fl oz) fish or light
    chicken stock

½ tsp saffron threads,
    steeped in 2 tbsp hot water

4 tbsp sherry vinegar

4 tbsp clear honey

2¾oz raisins, plumped
    up in hot water

2oz pine nuts, toasted

leaves from a medium bunch
    of cilantro, roughly
    chopped

1 Heat about 3 tbsp olive oil in a frying pan with a lid, season the fish and quickly sauté it on each side until it's golden. You just want to color the outside, not cook the fish through. Remove the fish and reserve it.

2 Now cook the onion in the same pan, with 2 tbsp more oil if you need it, until just beginning to turn golden. Add the cinnamon and chili and cook for another couple of minutes. Pour on the stock and add the saffron, vinegar, and honey. Drain the raisins and add those, too, along with the pine nuts. Season and throw in half the cilantro. Bring to the boil, then turn down and simmer for about 10 minutes.

3 Put the fish on top of the onion mixture, spooning some of the juices over it. Cover the pan and cook on a very low heat for another 8 minutes or so, or until the fish is cooked through. Serve immediately with the rest of the cilantro.

"Thy lips, O my spouse, drop as the honeycomb: honey and milk are under thy tongue; and the smell of thy garments is like the smell of Lebanon."

THE SONG OF SOLOMON

PEARL DIVERS' RICE

This dish, from Bahrain, is based on a recipe in Tess Mallos's encyclopedic work, The Complete Middle East Cookbook. *She explains that the dish got its name because pearl divers discovered they could dive more often, and with fewer ill-effects, if they had eaten something sweet (to maintain their blood-sugar level) and packed with carbohydrates. This dish provided everything they needed, though I wouldn't recommend going 130 feet under to test it.*

The original recipe is even sweeter than this, but I'd advise that you start off with the quantity of honey I've suggested to see how you like it. It's a haunting, tantalizingly perfumed dish, lovely with roast or grilled lamb or a herby lamb stew. As with some other Middle Eastern rice dishes, you have to cook it so that the rice forms a dark-brown crust, thought to be the best bit, at the bottom of the pan.

serves 4 as a side dish

8oz basmati rice

½ tsp saffron threads,
    steeped in 2tbsp hot water

1 tbsp rose water

seeds of 3 cardamom
    pods, crushed

4 tbsp clear honey

2¾oz butter

4 tbsp olive oil

salt and black pepper

1 Wash the rice in a sieve until the water is clear, then soak it for a couple of hours. Bring a pan of water to the boil and tip in the drained rice. Cook it for about 4 minutes, until the outside of the grain is softening but the inside remains hard.

2 While the rice is cooking, mix the saffron with the rose water and the crushed cardamom.

3 Drain the rice, rinse it with warm water and tip it into a bowl.

4 Stir the honey through the warm rice while you heat the butter and oil in a saucepan. When the fats are sizzling, add the honeyed rice and let it cook for a couple of minutes. Add the saffron, cardamom, and rose water mix, season with salt and pepper, and stir everything together.

5 Make three holes in the rice with the end of a wooden spoon. Wrap the pan lid in a clean dish towel, being sure to fold the edges underneath, and cover the pan. Turn the heat right down. Let the rice cook for about 15 minutes. Put the cooked rice in a serving dish and scrape the crusty bits off the bottom of the pan. Either stir the crusty bits through the rice or put them on the top. Serve immediately.

ADAM'S CAFE'S NORTH AFRICAN PICKLES

My craving for North African food is not, sadly, sated by frequent trips to Marrakesh. For my fix I head to Adam's Café, in the wilds of West London, where Frances and Abdel Boukraa run a regular "caff" during the day, transforming it into a den of couscous-eating and flower water-sprinkling at night. The pickles, put on your table as soon as you sit down, are one of the highlights. I persuaded them to part with their recipe and this is my version of it. It is not a true pickle so it won't keep indefinitely, but it will be fine in the refrigerator for about four weeks.

fills a 2 pint (32fl oz) jar

½ cucumber

2 tbsp coarse salt

3 carrots, peeled

1 onion, roughly chopped

1 red pepper, deseeded
   and chopped

1 very small head of cabbage,
   about the size of a head of
   radicchio, chopped

5½ oz olives, a mixture of
   black, violet, and green

1 lemon

2¼ cups (18fl oz) olive oil

2¼ cups (18fl oz)
   white-wine vinegar

leaves from 3 sprigs
   thyme, chopped

1 tsp dried oregano

1 tbsp caraway seeds, ground

1 tbsp coriander seeds

2 tbsp *harissa* (*see* p19)

1 Cut the cucumber into rounds, about an eighth of an inch thick, and put them in a small, non-reactive bowl. Sprinkle them with the salt and put them in the refrigerator for 2 hours. Drain them of the water that has leached out, then rinse. Gently pat them dry and put them at the bottom of a 2 pint (32fl oz) jar.

2 Cut the carrots into rounds, about the same thickness as the cucumber, and add these to the jar, together with the rest of the ingredients. Mix everything well to make sure you distribute the spices.

3 Cover and leave for a few days at room temperature, shaking the jar from time to time. After that, put your pickles in the refrigerator.

"*Empty pickle jars line*
the bottom of the pantry
gossiping in vinegar.
They await the alchemist's blessing
eager to join the consecrated
vessels amassed above,
flush with tarragon and mint
saffron and thyme..."

ARASH SAEDINIA, *A WORLD BETWEEN*

EGGPLANTS WITH MINT

Sweet, sour, and Sicilian.

*serves 4 as a side dish or as
part of an antipasto*

3 eggplants

olive oil

salt and pepper

FOR THE DRESSING

1 tsp white-wine vinegar

1 tbsp balsamic vinegar

2 garlic cloves, crushed

1 tsp superfine sugar

50ml (2fl oz) extra-virgin olive oil

a good handful of mint
    leaves, torn

1 Cut the top off the eggplants and cut them lengthwise into slices, about a quarter-inch thick. Paint them on each side with olive oil and season them.

2 Whisk all the dressing ingredients together with some salt and pepper.

3 Heat a griddle until very hot. Cook the eggplants to get a good color on each side, then turn the heat down so they can cook through.

4 Put the eggplants onto a serving platter and dress, while still hot, with the vinaigrette.

5 These are best if you leave them to soak up the dressing for a few hours, and then serve them at room temperature.

FRUITS IN HONEY AND MUSCAT WITH FROZEN YOGURT AND GLASS WAFERS

This dish can obviously be simplified by losing some of its components – the fruit is still fragrant and elegant served with plain Greek yogurt instead of the frozen kind. But it's an easy ice to make, and its tartness goes well with the shards of burnt sugar and the honeyed Muscat syrup.

Use French or Australian Muscat, Italian Moscato or the Greek dessert wine which goes by the gorgeously mellifluous name of Mavrodaphne.

serves 4-6

6 apricots

3 peaches or nectarines

5½oz sweet, ripe melon

1¼ cups (10fl oz) Muscat wine,
   or other sweet wine

¼ cup (2fl oz) water

5 tbsp orange-blossom honey

2 tsp orange-flower
   water (optional)

FOR THE FROZEN YOGURT

1¾ cups (14fl oz) Greek yogurt

4 tbsp confectioner's sugar

FOR THE WAFERS

vegetable oil

3½oz superfine sugar

1¼oz pistachios, very
   roughly chopped

1¼oz slivered almonds, toasted

1 Halve the apricots and peaches and remove the stones. Leave the apricots as they are, but cut each peach half into four even slices. Remove the peel and seeds from the melon and cut the flesh into chunks.

2 Put the Muscat, water, and honey into a saucepan and bring to the boil, stirring from time to time to help the honey melt. Turn this down to a simmer and poach the apricots and peaches very briefly. The amount of time this will take depends on the ripeness of the fruit. It's a good idea to cook each fruit separately and then remove it with a slotted spoon into a serving bowl. Keep checking the fruit as it is poaching – it may need as little as 2 minutes' cooking time. The melon doesn't need any cooking; just add it to the bowl of cooked fruit.

3 When you've finished poaching the fruit, boil the syrup until reduced by a third, then set it aside to cool. Once it's at room temperature, pour the syrup over the fruit. Taste and add the flower water if you want to. Chill the whole thing.

4 To make the frozen yogurt, simply stir the yogurt and sugar together. Churn in an ice-cream maker or still-freeze, whipping the mixture in a food processor, or by hand, a couple of times during the freezing process.

5 For the wafers, lightly oil a baking tray and melt the sugar with 4 tbsp of water over a medium heat. When the sugar has melted, boil it until it becomes a light caramel color, then add the nuts. When the sugar turns a deep caramel color, quickly pour the caramel onto the baking sheet, moving the sheet around so that the caramel sets in a thin sheet. Once it is cool and hard, break it up into large jagged pieces and serve with the frozen yogurt and fruit.

"Honey is the saliva of the stars." PLINY

"Spain frightened you. Spain

Where I felt at home. The blood-raw light,

The oiled anchovy faces, the African

Black edges to everything, frightened you"

TED HUGHES, "YOU HATED SPAIN", *BIRTHDAY LETTERS*

OF SEA AND SALT

ANCHOVIES, BOTTARGA, AND SALT COD

You know those late-night cravings you get? The ones which compel some people to consider trading their granny for a tub of Ben and Jerry's ice cream or a bag of hot buttery popcorn? Well, my cravings can be sated by slivers of rosy-pink flesh eaten straight from the can, the olive oil dripping inelegantly down my chin. My fix? Anchovy filets. They provide a bolt of such intense salty fishiness that my taste buds, previously in a frenzy of expectation, are calmed and satisfied. I may look like a Spanish fisherman, but I sigh contentedly and go back to watching the late-night movie.

Salted anchovies and salt cod are synonymous with the Mediterranean, conjuring up visions of blue and red painted boats, fishermen emptying throngs of silver fish onto the harbor, and black-clad old ladies tending terracotta pans, the pungent smell of their contents drifting up towards a statuette of the Blessed Virgin perched over the stove. Salt cod is almost a religious icon. It's the *fiel amigo* or "faithful friend" of the Portuguese, and in Spain a person of importance is known as *el que corta la bacalao* or "he who cuts the salt cod". Cod has sustained the Christian Mediterranean through centuries of Lent, but the fish doesn't actually come from the region; it has always been caught in the Atlantic and North Sea by the British, Irish, French, Scandinavians, Portuguese, and Basques. The Basques were catching – and then salting – cod in the waters near Newfoundland before the Americas had been "discovered", but since they valued fish over land, they kept quiet about where it came from.

Outside the Mediterranean and West Indies, salt cod is harder to sell. It has the grey-white color of overwashed underwear, looks like part of a corset, and smells like old socks. And anyway, who wants to eat salty fish? The thing is, if salt cod has been properly soaked, it shouldn't be unpalatably salty. Its character will be different from that of ordinary cod – its flavor distilled, its fishiness deepened – but it tastes less salty than anchovies. The American food writer Colman Andrews has written, in his book *Catalan Cuisine*, that the difference between salt cod and fresh cod is akin to that between fresh pork and cured pork: salt cod is a kind of bacon of the sea. Soak salt cod for two days, changing the water three times each day, then taste a bit – the fish should only be slightly salty. After that, it's easy to use. It's often served as salt-cod fritters or in a rough purée. The French make *brandade de morue*, blending poached salt cod, garlic, warm olive oil, milk, and sometimes a little potato. Italians have their own version of this purée, *baccalà mantecato*, which is made in much the same way. Pile spoonfuls of it on toasted *croûtes* and drizzle with olive oil for an appetizer.

You can even eat salt cod raw, once it's been soaked. Catalans eat thumb-thick shreds of it in a salad with tomatoes, olives, and strips of pepper. But my favorite raw treatment is paper-thin slices, moistened with strong extra-virgin olive oil and lemon, topped with very finely chopped garlic and parsley. For this kind of dish, and any dish in which you want to end up with large pieces of fish, buy salt cod taken from the middle of the fish – that's the thickest and meatiest part. In Portuguese shops you'll find about a dozen different grades; elsewhere you'll probably have the choice of the middle bit or the more gelatinous, stringy bits from the tail end, which are fine for puréeing.

Fresh anchovies are so beautiful – shimmering slivers of quicksilver – that it seems a shame not to eat them as they are. But once they're beheaded, gutted, and layered with salt crystals, they're even better. Their mild white flesh turns pale pink and develops a rich, deep flavor, fishy and meaty at the same time. You see them in glass jars or round cans in which their salt-encrusted bodies lie arranged like the spokes of a wheel. Just wash the fish gently, pull away the backbone, and pat them dry. Use them as they are or cover them with olive oil and keep them in the fridge for up to two weeks.

Most food writers tell you to buy these salted anchovies, but I actually prefer anchovies packed in olive oil, as long as they are really good quality. These have already gone through the salting process, but someone else has taken the trouble to rinse and filet them before slipping them into their olive oil bath. The oil softens the salt, the anchovies flavor the oil, and they both have a wonderful unctuous limpidity. Anchovies and olive oil were made for each other. Packed in cans, anchovies become one of the greatest convenience foods invented. Just peel back the lid and there, with a thick slice of country bread and a few tomatoes, is your lunch. Or try something a little more complicated – chop the filets and add them to a vinaigrette with parsley and crushed garlic to pour over sliced tomatoes, warm waxy potatoes or slivers of roast red pepper, or mash half a dozen filets with softened butter and rosemary or a scoopful of crushed black olives for a savory butter to melt over beef or lamb steaks.

Despite their strong identity, anchovies enhance other flavors. They make you appreciate the mild: try eating halved hard-boiled eggs with spoonfuls of puréed anchovy; they dance enticingly with the sweet: mix them with slow-cooked onions, peppers, and tomatoes; and they meld with and deepen the meaty: stuff anchovy halves along with slivers of garlic into a leg of lamb and you'll see what I mean.

Bottarga, the dried and salted roe of grey mullet or tuna, is a luxury that is eaten in Turkey, Egypt, France, and Italy. The aged version, popular in Sicily, is dark-brown in color and more solid and compact in texture. It's usually grated, smells like rotten fish, and, frankly, is not my cup of tea. The younger version, sold in a moulded sausage shape, is easier to find and delicious. It's the coral-brown color of the darker patches of smoked salmon and is served in fine curling slices that have a dense, almost waxy texture. Like anchovies, *bottarga* has an intense, salty fishiness which is perfect with mild flavors (try it with pasta and bread) and delicate salad leaves. It doesn't need to be cooked; in fact, don't do anything to it. It could become addictive, especially if, like me, you get salt cravings. But keep it under control. Sating late-night munchies with anchovies is definitely better for the bank balance.

CATALAN SALT COD AND PEPPER GRATIN

This was on my mind for years before I actually made it. I first ate it in a little seaside restaurant on the Costa Brava and was amazed at how subtle a dish made with salt cod and peppers could be. Rather than get it wrong, I thought it was better to keep the dish as a memory – then, thankfully, my attempt at recreating it worked. It's rich and creamy, with only a trace of the pungency that salt cod can have.

serves 8 as an appetizer,
4 as a main course

1½lb salt cod

2 bay leaves

1 onion, cut into thick slices

10 large red peppers, halved
    and deseeded

1lb potatoes, peeled

4 garlic cloves, crushed

1¼ cups (10fl oz) milk

1 cup (8fl oz) extra-virgin
    olive oil

salt and pepper

1 cup (8fl oz) heavy cream

a squeeze of lemon juice

1 Soak the salt cod for 48 hours, changing the water three times a day. When you want to cook the fish, drain it and fill a saucepan big enough to hold it with water. Add the bay leaves and onion and bring up to the boil. Turn the water down to a simmer and lower in the salt cod. Poach for 5 minutes, then turn off the heat and leave the salt cod to cool in the water.

2 Meanwhile, brush the peppers with a little oil and grill them, skin-side up, until blistering and black in parts. This will take 10-15 minutes. Leave them aside until they are cool enough to handle.

3 Boil the potatoes until they are tender, then drain them, put a clean cloth over them, and cover with a lid. Put the pan on a very low heat for 2-4 minutes just to dry the potatoes out a little, then roughly mash them before pushing them through a sieve or potato ricer.

4 Peel the skin off each of the peppers and put 8 of them (16 halves), in a single layer, into a lightly oiled ovenproof dish.

5 Take the salt cod out of the water and separate the flesh and skin from the bones. Put the flesh and skin in a food processor with the garlic and heat the milk and the olive oil separately. (The olive oil shouldn't be hot, just warm.) Purée the salt cod, adding the milk and oil a bit at a time. Add this to the mashed potato. Taste and add salt and pepper – yes, you will probably need salt, though I find every bit of salt cod varies.

6 To make the pepper sauce, heat the heavy cream to boiling. In a blender, purée the last 2 peppers with the heated cream. Taste and add salt, pepper and lemon juice.

7 Stuff each pepper half with the mashed salt cod, then pour the sauce over and around the peppers. Bake in an oven preheated to 350°F for 15 minutes, then grill very quickly until the top is slightly scorched. Serve as a main course with a spinach salad or warm green beans doused in olive oil and lemon, or as a starter with a few dressed leaves on the side.

SPAGHETTI WITH BOTTARGA, SHRIMP, PARSLEY, AND CHILI

Bottarga, *salted and dried grey mullet roe, isn't cheap, but a little goes a long way. Have this when you're feeling both lazy and rich — it's incredibly easy.*

serves 4

300g (10½oz) spaghetti

salt and pepper

1 onion, finely chopped

extra-virgin olive oil

1 tsp chili flakes

1lb 2oz raw shrimp,
    shelled and de-veined

a small bunch of flat-leaf
    parsley, finely chopped

juice of ½ lemon

3oz bottarga, shaved

1 Cook the spaghetti in plenty of boiling, salted water while you make the sauce.

2 Sauté the onion in 2 tbsp of the olive oil until soft and just turning golden. Add the chili flakes and shrimp. Stir the shrimp and onion around until the shrimp turn pink and are cooked — it will take about 2 minutes. Add the parsley and lemon juice.

3 Drain the spaghetti and, while still warm, season it with salt and pepper and moisten with a good slug of extra-virgin olive oil. Add the shrimp mixture and tip it into a heated serving bowl. Scatter with the shaved *bottarga*, toss lightly and serve.

PASTA WITH TWO ANCHOVY SAUCES

These are two of the most delicious pasta sauces I know. Both are from the heavenly Sicilian repertoire, and both are pretty much based on pantry basics. The first dish, a blend of salty and sweet, perfumed with saffron, reeks of Arab invention. Similar pasta dishes are made with fresh sardines or cauliflower, and I sometimes add one or other of those to this dish. The Pasta with Anchovies and Breadcrumbs (overleaf) is a dish I have eaten in a restaurant called Jonico in Syracuse, Sicily, and is so purely anchovy that you could be eating the sea. I make these sauces with run-of-the-mill anchovies when I have nothing else, but do try them with top-quality ones (such as Ortiz) for a sublime experience.

PASTA WITH ANCHOVIES, PINE NUTS, CURRANTS, AND SAFFRON

both recipes serve 4-6

¼ tsp saffron threads

2oz currants

2¼oz (drained weight)
   anchovy filets in oil

milk

14oz spaghetti or bucatini

salt and pepper

1 fennel bulb

½ cup (4fl oz) extra-virgin
   olive oil

2¾oz pine nuts

2 garlic cloves, crushed

a large bunch of flat-leaf
   parsley

1½oz fried breadcrumbs
   (*see* p70)

1 Mix the saffron with 1 tbsp of just-boiled water. Cover the currants with hot water and leave to plump up. Soak the anchovies in a little milk for about 15 minutes.

2 Cook the pasta in plenty of boiling salted water. Trim the fennel bulb, reserving any little feathery fronds, and remove the tough outer leaves. Quarter and cut the central core from each piece. Chop the rest into little cubes. Drain the anchovies and the currants.

3 Heat 2 tbsp of the olive oil in a saucepan and gently sauté the fennel for a couple of minutes. Add the pine nuts and cook until pale gold, then add the garlic and cook for another 30 seconds without coloring it. Pour on the rest of the olive oil, then add the currants, anchovies, and any fennel fronds. Cook over a gentle heat, stirring to help the anchovies melt.

4 Roughly chop the parsley and throw it into the pan, followed by the saffron and some pepper. Stir everything together and cook for another half-minute. Drain the pasta and toss it together with the sauce and the fried breadcrumbs. Pour on a further slug of extra-virgin olive oil if you want everything to be a little more moist, and serve.

"With a well-prepared anchovy sauce, one might eat an elephant."

GRIMOD DE LA REYNIERE

ALMANACH DES GOURMANDS

PASTA WITH ANCHOVIES AND BREADCRUMBS

4½oz (drained weight)
  anchovy filets

milk

1lb spaghetti or bucatini

a little salt

2¾fl oz extra-virgin olive oil

2 garlic cloves

½ tsp chili flakes

a large bunch of
  flat-leaf parsley

2¼oz fried breadcrumbs
  (*see* p14)

1 Soak the anchovies in a little milk for about 15 minutes. Put the pasta on to cook in plenty of boiling salted water.

2 Gently heat the olive oil – you mustn't get it too hot or it will spoil the flavor of the oil – and cook the whole garlic cloves for a couple of minutes, until golden. Discard the garlic and take the pan off the heat. Drain the anchovies, cut them up, and add them to the oil with the chili flakes. Heat gently, helping the anchovies melt by mashing them with a wooden spoon.

3 When the pasta is almost ready, roughly chop the parsley and gently reheat the anchovy sauce. You can incorporate a few tablespoons of the pasta cooking water into the sauce to stretch it a little if you want to. Toss the drained spaghetti with the sauce, parsley, and breadcrumbs, and serve.

RHÔNE FERRYMAN'S BEEF WITH CARMARGUE RED RICE

This is my version of brouffado, *a Provençal dish once served at the restaurant Le Vaccarès in the central square in Arles, which is now, sadly, no longer there. Dating from the 1940s, Le Vaccarès was an Arles institution. Eating there, among the dark wooden furniture and leather club chairs, one entered a different age. Their* brouffado *breathes of the past. You can imagine Hemingway, who used to hang out in Arles when he visited for the bullfighting, enjoying such a pungent, macho dish.*

serves 4

olive oil

2 tbsp balsamic vinegar

black pepper

1 bay leaf

4 sprigs thyme

6 cloves

2 strips orange rind

1¾lb beef (top round),
    plus fat for barding

1 onion, finely sliced

3 garlic cloves, finely chopped

3 tbsp capers, rinsed
    of vinegar, brine or salt

FOR THE RED RICE

½ onion, finely chopped

1 celery stick, diced

2 tbsp olive oil

10½oz red rice

3½ cups (28fl oz)
    chicken stock

salt and pepper

½oz flat-leaf parsley,

TO SERVE

8 anchovy filets in olive oil

milk

3 gherkins, finely chopped

2 tbsp extra-virgin olive oil

1 Make a marinade by mixing 4 tbsp of olive oil with the balsamic vinegar, pepper, bay, thyme, cloves, and orange rind. Put the joint of beef in the marinade, turning the meat over to make sure it's well-coated, then leave it to marinate overnight, or for at least 2 hours. Turn it every so often.

2 Take the meat out of the marinade and tie the fat around it with kitchen string. Put 3 tbsp of olive oil in a small casserole and brown the meat on all sides. Take the casserole off the heat. Add the capers to the casserole with the onion and garlic, the reserved marinade, and 7fl oz of water. Cover and cook in a slow oven – preheated to 300°F – for 1 hour 20 minutes. You need to baste the meat and turn it over a few times during cooking.

3 About 45 minutes before the meat is due to be ready, cook the red rice. Simply sauté the onion and celery in the olive oil until soft. Add the rice and cook for another couple of minutes. Add the stock, season, and bring to the boil. Turn down to a simmer, cover, and let the rice cook for about 45 minutes, by which time it will have absorbed all the stock. Red rice never cooks to softness, but retains a nutty bite. Stir half of the parsley into the rice. Soak the anchovies in a little milk and chop the gherkins.

4 When the beef is cooked, remove it from the oven and keep it warm. Skim the fat off the top of the juices, then reduce them slightly by boiling. Retain about 5 tbsp of the juice and put the rest back with the beef.

5 Drain the anchovies and gently heat them in the extra-virgin olive oil. Once they melt and break up into a purée, gradually add the reserved beef juice. The sauce shouldn't be too runny, so if you have too much meat juice add it back to the beef.

6 Carve the beef and put it on a platter with its juices. Pour the anchovy sauce over the top. Scatter with the gherkins and the rest of the parsley, and serve with the rice.

*"Its covering is composed
of two halves so joined
it's a pleasure to see:
like eyelids closed in sleep."*

ABU BAKR MUHAMMAD IBN AL-QUTIYYAH, "WALNUT",

POEMS OF ARAB ANDALUSIA

PLUNDERING THE STORES

ALMONDS, HAZELNUTS, PINE NUTS, PISTACHIOS, WALNUTS, AND DRIED FRUITS

The glass cases that run along the walls of the Middle Eastern grocery look as though they are filled with seashells, shards of flint, pebbles, and water-polished stones. With half-closed eyes, the image looks like an ancient mosaic, but it's actually nuts: shelled and unshelled, salted and unsalted, shiny and matte. An old man is busy talking to the cashier and eating pistachios, nonchalantly sticking his thumbnail into the little slit that Iranians call "the smile", then throwing the shell aside to join a trail of debris that, unlike sweet wrappers, you couldn't categorize as rubbish. He eats the nut, with its crimson- and rose-flushed coat, its interior as emerald as the youngest fava bean. The taste, a reference point for so many other foods (nutty pumpkins, nutty wild rice, nutty cheese), is sweet and earthy. It's a taste as old as olives, as ancient as grapes.

Although the mention of Mediterranean food conjures up images of tomatoes, peppers, and eggplants, it is nuts – grown for centuries before these other "Mediterranean" interlopers came from the New World – that really mark the cooking of the Middle East, North Africa, and the parts of Europe where the Arabs made them so popular: Spain and southern Italy. Here nuts are core ingredients, not just extras to be brought in at Christmas.

Walnuts are eaten with salt and glasses of *raki* in the cafés of Baghdad, while almonds are swallowed with slurps of dry fino sherry in the tapas bars of Andalusia. Everywhere, nuts are chopped, ground, and pulverized for sauces, soups, stews, stuffings, and pastries. Shoppers in Iran and Turkey can browse in specialist nut and dried-fruit shops, sifting through the many varieties of Iran's "green gold" (the Persian term for pistachios) or deliberating over their preferred type of walnut. Cooks in Catalonia will argue about whether you should use hazelnuts or almonds in a particular sauce and *picada* – a paste made of pounded nuts, wafers or toasted bread, garlic, parsley, and olive oil – is a brilliant centuries-old thickener and flavor enhancer for Catalan stews. Italians work with the basic pesto idea, substituting walnuts or almonds for the more expensive pine nuts, and *khoresht*, the sweet/sour stews of Iran, are rich with tart apricots or sour cherries and scattered with slivers of almond or pistachio.

Back in the Middle Ages, we all loved nuts, especially in "white foods", or blancmanges. The rich were fond of supping these creamy concoctions of chicken breasts pounded with milk, broth, almonds, sugar, and rose water. At times of religious observance, when cow and goat milk (as well as meat) were forbidden, blancmanges could easily be made legitimate by using almond milk. It's impossible to be sure about influences, but you can still find a Turkish pudding, *tavuk gogsu*, made of pounded chicken breasts, sugar, cream, and rice flour, so the original blancmanges may have had their origins in this kind of Middle Eastern dish. Sweet blancmanges are still eaten today: *biancomangiare*, a thick Italian custard, is made with almond milk in parts of Sicily, and *eiviesseniques*, an Ibizan Christmas pudding, is a kind of creamy nut porridge.

Pastries and cakes from Brighton to Boston still depend on the subtle, aristocratic flavor of the almond, and little string bags of hazelnuts and walnuts make their annual appearance along with Santa Claus. But northern European and American cooks simply don't grind nuts to thicken sauces or pile them into pastries like they do in Spain, Italy, and the Middle East. Turkey and Greece have their syrup-drenched *baklava*, sugary-sweet layers of filo pastry, dense with honeyed walnuts. Moroccans eat flower water-soaked pastries stuffed with almonds or pistachios ground with melted butter. Spain and Italy have a seemingly endless array of nutty confections: innumerable brittle *biscotti*; cloud-light Sicilian egg and almond *fior di mandorle* or "almond blossoms"; Catalan potato- and nut-based wafers called *panellets*; and the ubiquitous Italian *amaretti*. The Spanish have their almond-dense nougat, *turrón*, and countless almond tarts and cakes; the Italians have *torrone* and their revered marzipan or *pasta reale* (royal paste), as it is known there. Sicilian *pasticceria* are stuffed with marzipan sweets, sculpted and painted into every fruit and vegetable shape imaginable.

Fancy a cold glass of almond milk? In Sicily it's as easy to buy as a Coke. And a transportable summer breakfast of almond *granita* couched in a warm baby brioche is not a once-in-a-while treat: you can have it every day on the way to the office.

The great thing about nuts is that they are common, and yet they have the power to produce the unusual. There are few places where you can't pick up a bag of nuts on the way home from work. Once in the kitchen you can make *tarator*, a kind of Middle Eastern pesto, by crushing walnuts, hazelnuts or pine nuts with garlic and olive oil until you have a purée. Dip raw vegetables into it, use it to dress warm green beans, or serve it with roast chicken. Alternatively, create a "modern" version by processing pine nuts with roasted garlic and parsley while trickling on extra-virgin olive oil — drizzle this over seared lamb chops or grilled peppers and you'll be glad you didn't settle for the frozen dinner from the supermarket.

With a bag of fresh nuts, some garlic, and a packet of herbs, you can always make a pesto, and you don't have to stop at Genoa. Use half walnuts and half pine nuts, add parsley as well as basil, and you have *castelnuovo* pesto. Use almonds, oregano and tomatoes and you have Sicilian pesto. Try walnuts alone, adding a little cream cheese and a couple of tablespoons of cream before stirring in the Parmesan and you have *salsa di noci*. Nuts may, by nature, be crunchy, but pulverize them and they willingly amalgamate with and absorb other flavors, turning into grainy or silky-smooth unguents.

Add dried fruit to dishes containing nuts, and you can conjure with sweet and sour. Dot a bowl of rice or couscous with slivers of pistachios, eyes of toasted almonds, and tart sweet chunks of dried apricots, or cook a couple of pounds of lamb with raisins, pine nuts, and honey. You will have left a dull winter night far behind. Stuff a sardine with breadcrumbs mixed with orange, parsley, pine nuts and currants and you are somewhere warm, somewhere exotic, somewhere Sicilian. Add pine nuts, raisins, and a good slug of sherry to the pan halfway through roasting a chicken and you'll find yourself in Andalucía. And these are just a few of the better-known uses for nuts and dried fruits. You could also stuff a fish, Lebanese-style, with chopped walnuts, pomegranates, garlic and cilantro or mix green olives, chopped lemon flesh, mint, olive oil, and walnuts to make a Turkish salad-cum-salsa for kabobs.

I tend to use nuts and dried fruits in savory dishes more than I do in sweet ones, but I am always amazed at the range of impromptu, no-fuss desserts I can churn out with them. It takes 15 minutes to make a Turkish-inspired dish of dried cherries, simmered in a syrup with a hint of rose water, to go with rice pudding. Or what about a compote of dried prunes, apricots, and apples, flavored with cardamom and scattered with pomegranate seeds? I keep a big jar of raisins steeped in Marsala – an idea stolen from a restaurant in Umbria – for a quick ice-cream sauce, and a dish of dried apricots macerated in Muscat or, if you want to be extravagant, Sauternes, always feels luxurious. Stash a box of Spanish *turrón* at the back of a cupboard so you can stir chunks of it into a tub of good-quality vanilla ice cream. Add slivers of almonds and pistachios to a saucepan of caramel, pour on a greased baking sheet, and break the result into glassy shards to eat with ices. And while I have never liked marzipan on Christmas cake, I love little chunks of it baked in halved plums or pears or, mixed with chocolate and walnuts, stuffed into figs or prunes and poached in a rich port syrup.

To buy nuts, it's worth going to a Middle Eastern or Italian store, which has a good turnover. Nuts don't keep well (walnuts and pine nuts, in particular, go musty and rancid quickly), so buy them in small quantities. They always taste better freshly shelled but, let's be realistic, you're probably only going to do this if you're eating them round a table with friends at the end of a meal. For cooking, try to buy nuts in their skins and blanch them yourself – just soak in boiled water for 15 minutes, then rub the skins off with a tea towel and leave the nuts somewhere warm to dry. If you want flaked or knibbed almonds, they're easier to cut while they're still wet. If you don't have time for any of this, a little toasting brings out the flavor of the most mundane nut – I always do it with nuts destined for a salad. But unless you're happy to cook with sawdust, avoid buying nuts ready-ground. It takes just a bit of effort to bung blanched almonds into the food processor. You won't be able to grind them as finely as the shop-bought type, and you have to process them in small bursts or they become oily, but the flavor is so much better.

Try specialist shops for dried fruits, too; you'll get a wider variety than in the supermarket. "Raisin" is the name given to different types of dried grapes, ranging from the mundane varieties to the lusciously burnt-sugar-tasting ones such as Muscatel. Specialist shops can at least tell you the country of origin, if not the grape variety. Sultanas are usually dried seedless green grapes, less sweet and less complex in flavor than raisins. Currants, whose beady little bodies I ignored until I began to cook Sicilian food, are a particular variety of small black grape originally grown in Corinth in Greece. They are essential in some Sicilian dishes, such as pasta with anchovies, pine nuts and currants, where you want only small bursts of sweetness.

Nuts and dried fruit define the food of the Middle East and parts of the Mediterranean just as much as spices. They may be everyday ingredients, but as long as you have walnuts, almonds, and raisins in your kitchen, you will always be able to experience the exotic – without going anywhere.

SARDINES BECCAFICO

Sarde a beccafico is yet another sweet-sour Sicilian dish. There's hardly a restaurant in Palermo that doesn't serve it. Some versions have grated pecorino in the stuffing, others even have extra sugar (though that's taking the sweet thing a bit too far, even for me). The dish got its name, apparently, from the beccafico, a little songbird that eats only figs and so ends up as sweet as these sardines.

*serves 4 as a appetizer or
light main course*

12 sardines

1 orange, finely sliced

12 bay leaves

extra-virgin olive oil

FOR THE STUFFING

1 onion, finely chopped

60ml (4 tbsp) olive oil

2 garlic cloves, minced

8 anchovy filets in oil, soaked
    in milk for 15 minutes

2oz raisins, soaked in
    hot water and drained

1½oz pine nuts, toasted

2½ tbsp capers, rinsed of salt,
    vinegar or brine,
    and chopped

2¼oz white breadcrumbs

juice and rind of 1 orange

juice of ½ lemon

a small bunch of flat-leaf
    parsley, chopped

black pepper

1 Scale the sardines and gut them. Cut the head off each one. Break the backbone at the head end and gently pull it out, taking the bones with it. Wash all the fish well and refrigerate until you're ready to stuff them.

2 For the stuffing, sauté the onion in the olive oil until soft and translucent. Add the garlic and cook for another 1½ minutes. Drain the anchovies, chop them, and add them to the pan with all the other stuffing ingredients. Season with pepper – you don't need salt because of the capers and anchovies.

3 Stuff each sardine, then roll it up, head to tail, and place it in an ovenproof dish big enough to hold all the fish snugly, with the tail sticking up. If you can't be bothered to do this, or you find it difficult, just lay the stuffed fish side-by-side in the dish.

4 Halve the orange slices and put them and the bay leaves in between the fish. Pour a little extra-virgin over everything and bake in an oven preheated to 350°F for 20-25 minutes. The sardines are usually served at room temperature in Sicily, but I prefer them hot.

"The swordfish and tuna were flanked by many smaller fish, striped mackerel and fat sardines... I remember how the diffused red light of the market enhanced the translucent red of the big fishes' flesh and the silver glitter of the smaller ones' skins."

PETER ROBB, *MIDNIGHT IN SICILY*

GRILLED SWORDFISH WITH SALSA ROMESCO

Salsa Romesco is a great partner for all kinds of grilled fish, particularly the more meaty ones, although the Spanish also eat it with pork and lamb. There are as many recipes for it as there are cooks in Spain: the following is just my version but I, obviously, like it best. It's famously consumed in large quantities at the calçot *festival held every year in Catalonia, a deliciously messy affair where hundreds of* calçots *(which are like big, fat spring onions) are char-grilled until black, stripped of their skins, and dipped in this nutty sauce. You could char-grill baby leeks or the biggest spring onions you can find and serve them with this dish or as a appetizer.*

You should really use ñora *peppers to make Romesco, but they're hard to find so I've substituted ancho chilies. Use four* ñora *peppers in place of the ancho chilies if you can get hold of them.*

serves 4

4 swordfish steaks

olive oil

salt and pepper

FOR THE SALSA

1½ dried ancho chilies

3 garlic cloves

olive oil

1 slice country bread
  (about 1½oz)

1oz shelled hazelnuts

a good 1oz blanched almonds

2 plum tomatoes

1 tsp soft dark-brown sugar

½ red pepper, deseeded

½ medium red chili,
  deseeded and chopped

½ tsp *pimentón de la Vera*
  (sweet smoked
  Spanish paprika)

¾ tbsp sherry vinegar

2¾fl oz extra-virgin olive oil

1 Cover the ancho chilies in very hot water and leave them to soak and plump up. Sauté two of the garlic cloves in a couple of tablespoons of oil until pale gold and reserve them. Discard the crusts, tear the bread into pieces, and sauté it in the garlicky olive oil until well colored. Toast the nuts in a dry pan until just browning. Set these aside.

2 Halve the tomatoes and sprinkle with the brown sugar. Brush the pepper with a little olive oil, then broil it with the tomatoes until the latter have caramelized on top and the pepper is blistered and black in patches. When the pepper is cool enough to handle, peel the skin off and put the flesh into a food processor with the tomatoes, bread, and both the raw and the sautéed garlic.

3 Drain the anchos, reserving a little of the soaking liquid. Cut the anchos open and remove and discard the seeds. Put the anchos and 2 tbsp of the soaking liquid into the food processor, then add all the other salsa ingredients, except the extra-virgin olive oil. Season with salt and pepper. Turn the machine on and gradually add the oil in a steady stream. Taste for seasoning – you may want a little more sherry vinegar or salt.

4 Brush the swordfish with olive oil and season. Cook on a very hot griddle, coloring both sides, and then turn the heat down so that the fish can cook in the center. Serve with the salsa.

LAMB AND MINT PILAF WITH TURKISH CHERRY HOSAF

Hosaf is a kind of moistener for eating with pilafs and is also eaten as a dessert. It's sweet and fragrant and won't be to everybody's taste, but I love it. You can also make it with plums, apricots or sultanas (golden raisins). A Turkish friend of mine advises keeping it in the refrigerator, where it not only lasts for ages but brings an immediate blast of cold sweetness to your meal. Use it to anoint pilafs dotted with lamb, fish, even feta, and flavored with mint or dill. I also like it with kabobs, though that's not strictly Turkish.

serves 4

olive oil

1lb 9oz lamb from the leg or
    shoulder, excess fat removed,
    cut into chunks

1 onion, chopped

1 tsp ground cinnamon

unsalted butter

6oz bulgar wheat

1½ cups (12fl oz) stock or water

leaves from a small bunch of
    mint, torn

Greek yogurt, to serve

garlic cloves, to serve

FOR THE *HOSAF*

7oz superfine sugar

1⅛ cups (9fl oz) water

½ cinnamon stick

7oz dried sour cherries

juice of ½ lime

1 tbsp rose water

1 Make the *hosaf* first, as it needs to be eaten cold. Put the sugar, water, and cinnamon in a saucepan and gently heat. Stir from time to time to help the sugar melt. When the sugar has dissolved, bring the liquid up to the boil and boil for 5 minutes. Add the cherries and continue to cook over a low heat for about 15 minutes, then let the cherries cool. Remove the cinnamon and add the lime juice and rose water.

2 Heat 2 tbsp oil in a pan and brown the chunks of lamb all over. Remove the meat and set it aside. Add a little more oil to the same pan, and sauté the onion until soft and starting to color. Add the cinnamon and cook the spice with the onion for about a minute. Put the meat back into the pan, just cover with water or stock, and bring everything to the boil. Turn the heat down very low and let the lamb cook gently for about half an hour.

3 Melt a good knob of butter and ½ tbsp of oil in a heavy-bottomed saucepan. Stir the bulgar wheat round in this for a few minutes until it is well coated. Add the lamb and its juices, plus about a cup of stock or water. (It is difficult to be prescriptive about the amount of stock as it depends how much liquid your lamb has produced. You want the bulgar to absorb the liquid as it cooks, so it's better to add a little at a time rather than have your pilaf swimming in liquid that it will never absorb.) Add a little more stock when necessary.

4 Bring everything to the boil, then immediately turn down the heat, wrap the pan lid in a clean dish towel, being careful to fold the corners underneath, and cover the saucepan. Cook for about 15 minutes, then take the pan off the heat. Fork the pilaf, add the mint, then cover again and let it sit for another 15 minutes.

5 Serve with the cherry *hosaf* and a bowl of Greek yogurt to which you have added some crushed garlic.

CHICKEN WITH MIGAS

This is based on a dish I once ate at the Zuni Café in San Francisco. It's a really unexpected mix of flavors, textures, and temperatures — cool leaves and fresh cilantro, toasted nuts, and sherry vinegar, warm bread soaking up hot chicken juices. A cross between a substantial salad and a roast chicken dinner, it's great as a not-too-heavy autumn lunch dish.

serves 4

1 bunch mixed herbs (parsley, chervil, chives, thyme)

a good 1oz butter

a good squeeze of lemon juice

salt and pepper

1 x 3 ¾ lb roasting chicken

1 tbsp balsamic vinegar

1 tbsp sherry vinegar

extra-virgin olive oil (optional)

FOR THE MIGAS
AND SALAD

13oz slightly stale country bread, crusts removed and torn into chunks

3 tbsp water

3 tbsp milk

2oz raisins

a little *saba* (*see* p103)

olive oil

4½oz spring onions, cut into 1¼ in lengths

2oz pine nuts

7oz lettuce leaves (mix of lamb's lettuce, baby spinach, and watercress)

a large bunch of cilantro

1 Roughly chop the herbs (remove the leaves from the stalks if you're using thyme) and mash them with the butter, lemon juice, and pepper. Loosen the chicken's skin, working your fingers carefully between skin and breast, down into the legs. Push chunks of the butter under the skin, massaging it in well, then put the chicken in the refrigerator for an hour. Season the bird inside and out, and roast in an oven preheated to 350°F for 1½ hours.

2 For the *migas*, moisten the bread with the water and milk and let it sit for about an hour. Put the raisins in a small pan and cover with a mixture of *saba* and a little water. Bring this to the boil, then immediately turn it off and let the raisins soak for half an hour.

3 Heat 2 tbsp of olive oil in a heavy-bottomed pan and cook the bread chunks on a high heat for about 30 seconds, then turn the heat down and cook the bread very slowly — it should take about 25 minutes. The chunks should be crisp and colored on the outside but moist on the inside.

4 Heat a little olive oil in another pan and sauté the spring onions for a minute. Add the pine nuts and sauté for another minute or so. Drain the raisins and add them, too. Set the mixture aside until you're putting the dish together.

5 Take the chicken out of the roasting pan, joint it into serving pieces, cover, and keep warm. Remove some of the excess fat from the roasting pan — there are lots of nice buttery juices that you don't want to lose, but get rid of some of the top layer of chicken fat by tilting the pan and spooning it off. Put the roasting pan on a medium heat on top of the stove and, when the juices start to bubble, add the vinegars. Stir well, scraping the pan to dislodge all the tasty bits stuck to it. Taste and decide whether you like it as it is, or you want to add a little extra-virgin olive oil — it really depends on how much juice the bird has produced and on what you fancy.

6 Throw the salad leaves, cilantro, *migas*, and spring onion mixture into a large shallow bowl, pour on the chicken juices and vinegar mix and toss lightly. Put the jointed chicken on top and serve.

CATALAN CHICKEN WITH PICADA

Picada is a miraculous thing; a centuries-old all-in-one thickener and flavor enhancer and one of the cornerstones of Catalan cooking. A slightly varying mixture of ingredients — fried bread, nuts, olive oil, spices, and herbs (and sometimes even dark chocolate) — is pounded together in a mortar and pestle and stirred into a dish five or ten minutes before the end of the cooking time. I just love the way it works, giving you a dish cloaked in thick juices without any recourse to flour, and impregnated with the most unexpected flavors that somehow seem to meld together. It's a good idea and one I use with not-thick-enough stews from other countries, too.

serves 4

8 chicken thighs, or a mixture
   of chicken joints, skin on
salt and pepper
olive oil
1 onion, finely chopped
4 plum tomatoes, finely
   chopped
2 garlic cloves, crushed
1¼ cups (10fl oz)
   chicken stock
a few sprigs of thyme
1oz pine nuts, toasted
2¾oz raisins, soaked in warm,
   dry sherry until plump
a good handful of flat-leaf
   parsley, roughly chopped

FOR THE *PICADA*

1 plain cookie (such as a
   graham cracker)
1oz country bread, fried in
   olive oil
1oz blanched almonds
5 tbsp dry white wine
3 tbsp extra-virgin olive oil

1 Season the chicken and brown it in about 2 tbsp of olive oil. You just want to give the bird a good color, not cook it all the way through.

2 Remove the chicken and set it aside. Add the onion to the same pan and cook until soft and translucent. Add the tomatoes and garlic and cook for another 2 minutes. Turn the heat down and gently cook the tomato mixture for a further 15 minutes until it's a thick purée. Add the stock and bring to the boil. Put the chicken back in the pan with any of the juices that may have leached out, plus the thyme, pine nuts and raisins. Turn the heat down and cook the chicken gently for about 25 minutes, or until it's just cooked through.

3 Make the *picada* by grinding the cookie, bread, and blanched almonds in a mortar and pestle (or process in a food processor, though I warn you it's hardly worth the washing up), gradually adding the white wine and olive oil.

4 Tip the *picada* into the chicken pan and stir everything together. Cook very gently for a further 5 minutes while the *picada* thickens the juices. Scatter with parsley and serve.

"Pleasures may be divided into six classes: to wit, food, drink, clothes, sex, scent, and sound. Of these, the noblest and most consequential is food."

MUHAMMAD IBN AL-HASAN AL-KATIB AL-BAGHDADI,
A BAGHDAD COOKERY BOOK

SALAD OF SWEET-AND-SOUR GRILLED CHICORIES WITH GOAT CHEESE

It's tempting to describe this as a bittersweet symphony, but I'll resist. Saba is sweet grape must and you should be able to find it in Italian delicatessens, but if you can't get hold of it, substitute a mixture of grape juice and balsamic vinegar.

Serves 4 as an appetizer or light lunch

1½oz raisins

saba

olive oil

balsamic vinegar

salt and pepper

1 large red onion

3 chicory *chicons*
    (Belgian endive heads)

1 head radicchio

leaves from a small bunch of
    flat-leaf parsley

¾oz pine nuts, toasted

5½oz goat cheese, crumbled

FOR THE DRESSING

1 tbsp balsamic vinegar

3 tbsp extra-virgin olive oil

juice of ½ lemon

salt and pepper

1 Put the raisins in a little saucepan and add just enough *saba* and water to cover (about half and half). Bring to the boil, then turn the heat off and let the raisins soak up the liquid for about half an hour.

2 Pour 3-4 tbsp of olive oil into a shallow dish and add a slug of balsamic vinegar, some salt, and pepper.

3 Heat a griddle. Cut the onion in half, and then cut each half into quarters lengthwise, producing half-moon shapes. Put each half-moon in the oil and vinegar mixture. Once the griddle is very hot, take the onions out of the mixture, shaking off the excess, and put them on the pan. Cook them on each side on a high heat, then turn the heat down and let them cook until they're beginning to soften. It doesn't matter if the sections fall apart. Set the onions aside.

4 Quarter each *chicon* of chicory and the head of radicchio. Put them immediately in the oil and vinegar mixture so they get a light coating. Heat the griddle again and sear these until charred and softened on the outside, but still uncooked on the inside.

5 Mix all the dressing ingredients in a large bowl. Toss the chicory, radicchio, onion, and parsley in the dressing, then divide them among four plates or put on a large serving platter. Drain the raisins and scatter these, the parsley, pine nuts, and goat cheese over the top. Serve at room temperature.

RAISIN AND SHERRY ICE CREAM

A far cry from rum-and-raisin. Use the fattest, best-quality raisins you can find. If you don't want to splurge out on Pedro Ximénez – a luscious, brown-sugar-tasting sherry – use another good-quality sweet sherry, though you'll have a less multifaceted result.

serves 6

1¾ cups (14fl oz) milk

1 vanilla pod, split

5 egg yolks

3½oz superfine sugar

3oz raisins, soaked in
    ½ cup (4fl oz) Pedro
    Ximénez sherry

1¼ cups (10fl oz)
    whipping cream

To serve

more Pedro Ximénez sherry

1 Put the milk in a pan and scrape the vanilla seeds into it, adding the pod too. Heat the milk to just below boiling point, then take it off the heat and leave the vanilla to infuse for 20 minutes.

2 Beat the yolks and sugar together until pale and creamy. Reheat the milk to just below boiling point, remove the vanilla pod, and pour the milk over the egg and sugar mix, stirring all the time. Put this mixture into a bowl set over a saucepan of simmering water and cook, stirring continuously with a wooden spoon, until the custard has thickened slightly. It should be thick enough to coat the back of your spoon. Let it cool.

3 Add the raisins and sherry to the custard. Whip the cream lightly and stir it into the mixture. Churn in an ice-cream machine. Alternatively, still-freeze the custard, beating by hand three or four times during the freezing process. Because of the raisins, you can't beat this ice cream in a food processor.

4 Serve with a little extra sherry poured over the top.

"...the shop always smelled right, not confused and stuffy but delicately layered: fresh eggs, sweet butter, grated nutmeg, vanilla beans, old kirsch, newly ground almonds..."

M.F.K. FISHER, *TWO TOWNS IN PROVENCE*

SICILIAN ALMOND GRANITA

This is as common in Sicily as vanilla ice cream is everywhere else. It's usually served with warm brioche on the side, or even spooned into warm baby brioche and eaten on the way to work. Do use good almonds.

serves 4

9oz blanched almonds

2½ cups (20fl oz) water

4½oz superfine sugar

amaretto liqueur,
   to serve (optional)

1 Put half the almonds and half the water in a blender and process them. You'll have to stop the machine and dig down into it several times to help loosen the almonds that get stuck around the blade.

2 Pour the almond milk into a large sieve lined with cheesecloth, placed over a bowl. Repeat this with the rest of the nuts and water.

3 Put the almond milk and the bowl in the refrigerator, and let the milk drip through into the bowl overnight. Help it along every so often by gripping the cheesecloth into a bag shape and squeezing out the liquid. The next day, squeeze out as much liquid as you can.

4 Add the sugar to the almond milk, mix it well, and pour it into a shallow container. Freeze, roughly forking through the slush to separate the crystals every so often. You should end up with rough, frozen shards.

5 Serve in frosted glasses, with a slug of amaretto poured over the top.

CHOCOLATE, HAZELNUT, AND SHERRY CAKE WITH SHERRY-RAISIN CREAM

Chocolate and sherry — a marriage made in heaven. Treat yourself to a glass of raisiny sweet Pedro Ximénez sherry to go with it...

serves 8

5oz dark (semi-sweet)
   chocolate

2¾oz unsalted butter

½ cup (4fl oz) dry fino sherry

6 medium eggs, separated

5¾oz superfine sugar

5½oz shelled hazelnuts,
   toasted and
   coarsely chopped

1 Grease an eight-inch diameter springform cake pan, and line the bottom with greaseproof paper.

2 Put the chocolate, butter, and sherry in a bowl and set it over a pan of simmering water. Heat until everything has melted, stirring from time to time to help it along. Let this cool.

3 Whisk the egg yolks with the sugar until glossy. Add the cooled chocolate mixture and 2½oz of the hazelnuts. Beat the egg whites until fairly stiff. Using a large metal spoon loosen the chocolate mixture with 1 big spoonful of egg white, then fold in the rest with the flour, cocoa, and salt.

a pinch of salt

2oz self-rising flour, sifted

2oz cocoa powder, sifted

confectioner's sugar
  for dusting

FOR THE CREAM

9oz raisins

1⅛ cups (9fl oz) oloroso
  sherry

1⅜ cups (11fl oz) heavy cream

4 tbsp Greek yogurt or
  fromage frais

4 tbsp confectioner's sugar

4 Pour into the prepared pan and bake in an oven preheated to 350°F for 50 minutes. Test the cake with a skewer and, if it comes out clean, it's done; otherwise leave it for another 5-10 minutes, but keep checking with a skewer. Leave the cake to cool in the pan for half an hour before turning it out.

5 To make the cream, heat the raisins in the sherry in a small saucepan. When the sherry is just under boiling point, turn the heat off and leave the raisins to plump up and cool.

6 Whip the cream and stir the yogurt and sugar into it. Add the raisins with their soaking liquid and check the sweetness.

7 Dust the surface of the cake with a little confectioner's sugar, then scatter the rest of the chopped hazelnuts on top. Finish with another light dusting of confectioner's sugar and serve with spoonfuls of cream.

"Guarded treasure, honeycomb partitions,

Richness of flavor,

Pentagonal architecture.

The rind splits; the seeds fall —

Crimson seeds in azure bowls…"

ANDRE GIDE, "THE LAY OF THE POMEGRANATE",

FRUITS OF THE EARTH

FRUITS OF LONGING

FIGS, QUINCES, POMEGRANATES, AND DATES

These are fruits that could turn a girl's head. Exotic, erotic, romantic, and elusive, they conjure up visions of hot sun, starry skies, silk canopies, and, let's be honest, sex. Figs are the sexiest of the lot. Purple ones are the color and texture of teenage love-bites, making you think of hungry kisses. One could even feel embarrassed handling figs in the wrong company. Soft and plump, it seems like they are just waiting to be discovered, so delicate that you have to touch them gently and eat them before too many little beads of nectar form around the flower end.

André Gide wrote that the fig had secrets, that it was a "Closed room where marriages are made" and D. H. Lawrence got straight to the point, "The Italians vulgarly say, it stands for the female part; the fig-fruit: The fissure, the *yoni*, The wonderful moist conductivity towards the center. Involved, Inturned, The flowering all inward and womb-fibrilled; And but one orifice."

Well, yes. Figs are unquestionably sensual. They even taste better if they've been sitting in the sun – never eat them straight from the refrigerator. Warmth seems to bring out their delicate flavor and make their skin all the softer on your lips. The fig's main drawback is that a good one is hard to find. Teasingly, they often promise more than they deliver. Their outside, be it black, purple, green or green-gold, gives no reliable clues. You may fall for a whole crate of beauties only to find every one disappointingly dry and tasteless. As in love, you have to hope. And keep trying…

When you do find perfect specimens, the best thing to do is leave them alone. Show off their lovely shape by serving a dozen of them on a platter at the end of a meal, or enhance their bloomy skin by setting them alongside a chalky goat cheese. Cut each fruit in four and open it like a flower, fill with mascarpone and drizzle with lightly warmed honey, or serve with raspberries and a honey or lemon ice cream. Or fill a cooked tart shell with honeyed cream and nestle quartered fresh figs on top. Simply dust with confectioner's sugar and you have a sugar-plum fairy of a dessert.

Slightly underripe figs are for baking and will give you sweet and savory dishes that are both elegant and earthy. Their little bodies really soak up juices and become fat with flavors: red wine with cinnamon, ginger, bay or thyme; white wine with a little cassis or rose water; orange juice with cardamom. Overripe figs – and they can get to this stage in the blink of an eye – are a good excuse to make a runny chutney, soft-set jam or the "spoonsweets" eaten in Greece and the Middle East (luscious fruits in syrup, eaten with little spoons and cups of thick, black coffee).

The beauty of the fig disappears, at least superficially, when it's dried. It becomes gnarled and misshapen. But dried figs have their own allure. Deep and rich, almost chocolatey, they make a great autumnal stuffing. Alternatively, bake dried figs as you would fresh ones and see how deliciously different the results are. Pairing dried figs with chocolate seems to restore some of their mystery; I can hardly think of a richer combination than dried figs and a good whack of cocoa solids. Strong, dark coffee with dried figs dipped in chocolate is a wickedly luxurious end to a wintry meal.

If the fig is young and untouched, the quince is all woman: curvaceous but graceful, mature, comfortable with herself and resilient to knocks, a big honey-sweet mamma of a fruit. I can never believe how satisfyingly weighty, nor how gorgeously rounded, quinces are in your hand. The Brussels bureaucrats would never be able to standardize these child-bearing hips to fit the EU's food regulations. But the quince has a mystique, just as the fig does, partly because it's so ancient and partly because it's so hard to get hold of. You're lucky if a friend with a tree gives you some, or if you come across a big golden mound of them in a market or a Middle Eastern shop. They're never around for long enough to take for granted. And that smell – honey, musk and roses ("the smell of my sweetheart's breath", wrote the Andalusian-Arab poet, Shafer ben Utman al-Mushafi) is hard to remember when the season is over.

All these fruits have to be handled properly to get the best out of them, but the quince needs the most work. Of course, you can fill a big bowl with them and enjoy their glow and fragrance for months, no cooking required, but you can't pick them up, toss them in the air, and sink your teeth into them. Their hard, acidic flesh has to be cooked, and cooked long and slow. Happily, they're so perfumed that you don't need to do anything complicated with them: poach them as you would pears, except for longer; parboil, slice, and bake them with raw pears covered in cream and sugar; add them to an apple sauce or a crumble. Raw, the flesh is as pale as an apple's; cooked slowly, it takes on a pinky hue that is beautiful beside a scoop of ice cream or sweetened Greek yogurt. And the quince's honeyedness is astonishing (the Romans called the quince *meli melum* or "honey apple"). Poached quinces taste like they've been steeped in Sauternes, so they're powerful enough to take on other distinctive flavors – cinnamon, cloves, star anise, saffron or even bay leaves and rosemary – and they're well able to take their place in spicy fruit and meat stews, such as the *tajines* of Morocco or the *khoresht* of Persia.

Quince cheese, a thick-set preserve made by cooking the whole fruit (skin, pips, and all), then sieving and simmering the resulting purée with an equal quantity of sugar, is made all over the Mediterranean and eaten as a sweetmeat with coffee. It's the Spanish, who call it by the lyrical-sounding name *membrillo*, who really know how to enjoy this. They serve it in thin slices, like bits of rosy-hued antique glass, beside chunks of strong cheese. You can find *membrillo* in delis, but it's not cheap – better to bag your quinces and spend a Saturday afternoon like some Andalusian mistress, stirring your pot of amber jelly and filling the house with the smell of heaven.

To me, dates mean rafts of cushions and desert nights, probably because the boxes in which the fruits arrived in our house at Christmas when I was a child were decorated with comic-book-style sketches of camels and Bedouin tents. They brought a whiff of the exotic that fancy chocolates never could. Imagine how delighted I was to discover that *deglat noor*, the name of one of the finest varieties, actually means "fingers of light". I used to think about eating these luscious fruits in the dark while listening to Maria Muldaur trilling through "Midnight at the Oasis". The earthbound reality was that I usually had rather dry dates, chopped up in brown-bread sandwiches for my school lunchbox. Well, they are very good with butter (and yogurt), as any desert nomad will tell you!

That tree of the sands, the date palm, drinks gallons of water from lakes below the ground, while the leaves provide sun canopies for trees of pomegranates, apricots and peaches. It's strange that we think of dates as a luxurious extra when they're a basic for Bedouins. They can survive for days in the desert on dates and camel milk. Small wonder that the fast of Ramadan is often broken with dates and a glass of water, or that dates are offered as a sign of friendship. There is a saying that the Bedouin spend their lives searching for "the two black ones": water and dates. Dates are, literally, life-giving.

All over the Arab world dates are made into exquisite sweetmeats, and the fruits bring the same rich orientalism to savory dishes that figs do. Dates are great with pigeon, lamb, and rice and are a revelation with oily fish. I've long since given up buying those Christmas boxes with their plastic spears, serving as harpoon and fake branch. Now I go for real branches of the fine, pale *deglat noor* or the plump mahogany beads called *medjool*. Treat them simply. Serve them at the end of a meal with salty cheese or *labneh*, yogurt, and honey, or with sliced oranges sprinkled with flower water and cinnamon. Or just offer mint tea and a tortoiseshell mix of dates on a plate: essence of the desert.

And then there's the pomegranate. "Beautiful color," sighs my friend Hattie. "Sin red." Modern Greek books on dreams do interpret pomegranates as a sign of temptation, sexual adventure, fertility, and even danger. They were, of course, the undoing of Persephone. Kidnapped by Pluto to be his bride in the underworld, she was allowed to return to earth providing she hadn't eaten anything in Hades. But she hadn't been able to resist the pomegranate. She had eaten six seeds, so for six months Persephone had to stay as Queen of the Dead in Hades while the earth mourned, only returning to earth for the remainder of the year. For the Greeks, the pomegranate is therefore double-edged: it embodies death and life. They eat the seeds in a kind of porridge of wheat and nuts at funerals but also smash the fruits on their doorsteps at New Year in anticipation of spring.

Pomegranates don't mean spring to me; they are winter and Christmas. With their leathery skin and regal little calyxes, they look like something one of the Magi would have given – or worn on his head. You don't even have to eat pomegranates to appreciate them. In December they hang like great baubles from trees in southern Italy, Turkey, and Greece, and arrive in markets with the Christmas lights. Those seeds – glassy lozenges of tart, sweet juice that burst against your tongue – are like festive jewels. Embedded in a beehive-like network of creamy pith, they can be deep garnet-red or pale rose-pink; nothing on the outside tells you which. Ask the vendor where the fruits are from: Spanish ones have paler seeds and are sweeter; Middle Eastern ones have redder seeds and a sourer flavor. Scattered on savory salads of chicory and salty cheese, or sweet ones of sliced oranges and ruby-pink grapefruit, pomegranates bring a little magic. Mixed with sugar and rose water, or orange juice and orange blossom water, they make an impromptu dessert worthy of *The Arabian Nights*. You can have something of pomegranates' tart, sour taste all year round with pomegranate molasses, an almost treacle-thick, dark-brown sauce made by boiling down the juice of the sourest specimens. A rich, acidic flavor enhancer for roasts, marinades, and dressings, no Middle Eastern kitchen would be complete without it.

SAUSAGES AND LENTILS WITH SWEET-AND-SOUR FIGS

The jammy figs in this dish are also good with pork chops, chicken or a plate of blue cheese.

serves 4

8 good-quality pork sausages

2 tbsp olive oil

2 medium onions

4½oz pancetta, cubed

9½oz green lentils, Puy
    or Umbrian

⅝ cups (5fl oz) dry white wine

2 cups (16fl oz) light
    chicken stock

salt and pepper

FOR THE FIGS

¼ cup (2fl oz) red-wine vinegar

¼ cup (2fl oz) balsamic vinegar

¼ cup (2fl oz) sherry vinegar

2¾oz superfine sugar

2-inch piece of cinnamon stick

12oz fresh figs

1 For the figs, put the vinegars into a saucepan and add the sugar and cinnamon. Dissolve the sugar over a low heat, then bring the liquid up to the boil. Turn the heat down immediately and simmer for 5 minutes. Halve the figs, add them to the vinegar, and simmer for another 5 minutes, until the mixture is slightly syrupy. It will thicken more as it cools.

2 Brown the sausages in the oil in a sauté pan: don't cook them through; just get a good color on the outside. Remove the sausages and set aside.

3 Peel the onions, halve them, and cut them from the root to the tip in crescent-moon shapes about a half-inch thick. Sauté the onions in the same pan in which you cooked the sausages until they're soft but not colored. Add the pancetta and cook for another 3 or 4 minutes on a higher heat — you want to give the pancetta and onion tips a good browning. Add the lentils and stir them round with the onions and pancetta. Pour on the wine and stock and bring to the boil. Season with salt and pepper, turn down to a simmer and add the browned sausages.

4 Cook the whole thing at a very gentle simmer on top of the stove for about 30 minutes, uncovered. The lentils should retain their bite, so don't let them get too soft, but different types and ages of lentils cook at different rates, so keep trying them. The stock and wine will become absorbed as the lentils cook. Add a little more stock or water if it looks like the mixture is becoming too dry. Serve from the pan with a bowl of the sweet and sour figs.

"We bought figs for breakfast, immense, thin-skinned ones. They broke in one's fingers and tasted of wine and honey. Why is the northern fig such a chaste, fair-haired virgin, such a SOPRANO? The melting contraltos sing through the ages."

KATHERINE MANSFIELD,
THE JOURNALS OF KATHERINE MANSFIELD

BREAST OF DUCK WITH POMEGRANATE AND WALNUT SAUCE

This dish (called fesenjan *in Iran) is one of the classics of Persian cuisine, though there the whole bird is used. This is a more modern, user-friendly version. The exquisite coupling of earthy walnuts and sweet/sour pomegranates makes a rich, autumnal sauce that is a good partner for duck or pheasant. In Iran, the sauce is also sometimes served with fish (it benefits from a handful of chopped cilantro in this case) and cooked eggplant slices.*

serves 4

4 duck breasts

5½ oz shelled walnuts

1 tbsp olive oil

½ onion, finely chopped

2 tsp ground cinnamon

2 tbsp pomegranate molasses

seeds of 2 pomegranates

1¾ cups (14fl oz) well-flavored
    chicken stock or duck stock

salt and pepper

a small bunch of mint, chopped

1 Toast the walnuts in a dry pan on top of the stove until they are just turning brown. Let them cool, then grind them in a food processor using the pulse button – you want to end up with a mixture that is partly ground and partly chunky. You could just bash the nuts in a plastic bag with a rolling pin if you don't want to hassle with the food processor.

2 Heat the oil in a shallow pan and gently sauté the onion until it is soft and turning golden. Add the cinnamon and stir for about a minute. Add the nuts, pomegranate molasses, and seeds and the stock. Stir everything together and bring to the boil. Turn down the heat and let the sauce cook for about 15 minutes until it's fairly thick.

3 To cook the duck breasts, season them on both sides and put into an ovenproof sauté pan, skin-side down, over a high heat. The fat under the skin will melt, providing oil in which to cook the breast. Quickly brown the duck breasts on both sides (the idea is just to color the breast, not to cook it through), then put them into an oven preheated to 400°F for about 7 minutes. After this time, check how well they are cooked by slightly cutting into the underside of the breast. You want to serve it like a rare steak.

4 Stir some chopped mint into the sauce at the last minute and serve alongside the duck breast, accompanied by simple side dishes such as rice and sautéed spinach.

"*Naked woman*

the pomegranate that broke

was full of stars."

GEORGE SEFERIS, "SIXTEEN HAIKU", *POEMS GIVEN*

SALAD OF MIDDLE EASTERN GRILLED CHICKEN, BULGAR WHEAT, AND POMEGRANATES

I love warm, main-course salads — you don't have to fool around trying to keep things hot and they make you feel so virtuous. This, as with every dish showered with pomegranate seeds, is unbelievably pretty. If you want to make it even more glamorous, use pigeon breasts instead of chicken (serve two breasts per person).

serves 4 as a main course,
6-8 as an appetizer
4 chicken breast filets,
    skinned
salt and pepper
1 medium red onion, finely
    chopped
3 tbsp olive oil
1 garlic clove, finely chopped
7oz bulgar wheat
1½ cups (12fl oz) chicken stock
2oz shelled walnuts
2 pomegranates
¾oz flat-leaf parsley,
    roughly chopped
¾oz cilantro, chopped
2¼oz watercress
Greek yogurt, to serve

FOR THE MARINADE
4 tbsp olive oil
1½ tbsp pomegranate syrup
1½ tbsp runny honey
½ tbsp ground cumin
2 garlic cloves, crushed

FOR THE DRESSING
juice of 1 lime
½ tsp runny honey
½ tsp *harissa* (see p19)
4 tbsp extra-virgin olive oil

1 Mix together all the ingredients for the marinade, seasoning with salt and pepper, and pour it over the chicken breasts. Marinate in the refrigerator, overnight if possible, or for at least a couple of hours.

2 To make the body of the salad, sauté the onion in the olive oil until just softening. Add the garlic, cook for another minute, and then add the bulgar wheat. Sauté the grains for a minute or two, turning them over in the oil, before adding the stock and some salt and pepper. Bring the stock to the boil, then turn the heat down to a very gentle simmer. Cover and cook the bulgar wheat until all the liquid has been absorbed. This will take about 15 minutes, but do give the wheat the odd stir to make sure it isn't sticking to the bottom of the pan. You should end up with a mixture that is fluffy and quite dry. Taste for seasoning, cover, and set aside.

3 Toast the walnuts in a dry frying pan and then break them into pieces. Halve the pomegranates and, holding them over a bowl, beat the fruit with a wooden spoon. The seeds should just spill out. Remove any coarse bits of yellow membrane still attached to them.

4 Take the chicken out of the marinade and grill it. Start on a very high heat, so that the outside gets nicely browned, basting with the marinade as it cooks. It will save clean-up time if you put the chicken on top of a piece of foil. Turn the chicken over halfway through, then lower the heat to finish the cooking. Cut each chicken breast into broad slices.

5 Make the dressing by whisking all the dressing ingredients together and seasoning with salt and pepper. While the chicken and bulgar wheat are still warm, mix them together with the herbs, watercress, nuts, and pomegranate seeds, reserving 3 tbsp of the seeds for garnish, and pour the dressing over the top. Divide the salad between four plates, or serve in a large shallow bowl topped with a spoonful of Greek yogurt and sprinkled with the reserved pomegranate seeds. Serve warm or at room temperature.

MOROCCAN LAMB AND QUINCE TAJINE

A rich, dark tajine — *the meat and fruit stews for which Morocco is so famous —
made a touch more elegant by the use of shanks instead of cubed lamb. This
predilection for fruit and meat combos probably came to North Africa with the
Arabs, and they probably picked it up from those masters of combining sweet and
sour, the Persians.*

serves 4

4 lamb shanks

3oz butter

½ tsp each of cumin and
   coriander seeds

1 tsp ground ginger

½ tsp cayenne pepper

3 garlic cloves, crushed

2 onions, roughly chopped

1¾ cups (14fl oz) stock
   or water

½ cinnamon stick

4 tbsp honey

1 large bunch cilantro,
   roughly chopped

salt and pepper

1 quince, peeled, quartered
   and cored

2 strips lemon rind

½ tsp saffron threads, dissolved
   in a little boiling water

1 Trim the lamb shanks of any excess fat and melt the butter in a casserole.
Grind the cumin and coriander seeds. Add these to the casserole with the
ginger, cayenne, garlic, onion, and lamb shanks and cook for about a minute.
The meat should not brown, but just get coated in the buttery juices. Pour
on the stock or water and add the cinnamon, half the honey and a third of
the cilantro leaves. Season. Bring to the boil, then turn the heat down very
low, cover, and cook the shanks for 1½ hours, or until the lamb is tender.

2 Put the quince in a saucepan with enough water just to cover. Add the
lemon rind and the remaining honey and bring to the boil. Turn down to a
simmer and poach the quince until tender — it really does have to be soft.

3 When the lamb is cooked, remove the shanks and keep them warm. Add
about 3 tbsp of the quince poaching liquid and the saffron to the meat juices
and reduce to a thickish sauce. Taste and adjust the seasoning. Slice the
quinces and add them to the sauce to heat through (for an even richer dish,
sauté the quince in butter until golden brown before adding it). Put the lamb
back into the casserole, together with any juices which have leached out.
Scatter fresh cilantro on top and serve with flatbread or couscous.

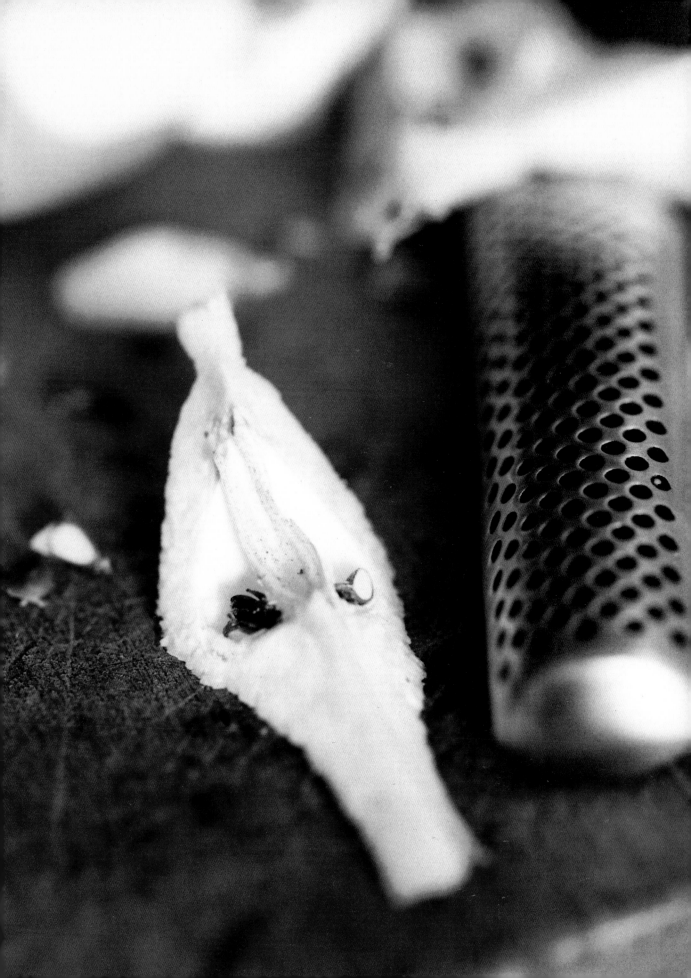

AUSTIN DE CROZE'S FIG ANCHOIADE

An intriguing recipe from the old gastronome, Austin de Croze, that never fails to incite one of those "guess what's in it" conversations.

serves 6

3 dried figs

1 red pepper

2 x 2oz cans anchovy filets in olive oil

2 garlic cloves

12 blanched almonds

a handful of flat-leaf parsley

1 tsp fennel seeds

black pepper

juice of ½ lemon

5/8 cup (5fl oz) extra-virgin olive oil

2 tsp orange-flower water

1 Soak the figs for 15 minutes in hot water, then drain. Halve and deseed the pepper, then grill until soft and starting to blister and turn black in patches. When the pepper is cool enough to handle, remove the skin.

2 Put everything, except the oil and orange flower water, into the food processor. Purée while adding the oil in a steady stream. Taste and add the flower water a spoonful at a time: this is in case you find it too perfumed – you may just want 1 spoonful.

3 That's it – and the flavor just keeps on getting better. Covered and kept in the refrigerator, this dish will be fine for about five days.

MUHAMARA

A sweet-sour, brick-red purée to eat with other little appetizer dishes as part of mezze or as an accompaniment to lamb or meaty fish such as swordfish.

Serves 8 as part of mezze

4 red peppers

1 small red chili

½ cup (4fl oz) extra-virgin olive oil

4½ oz shelled walnuts

2 garlic cloves

1oz dry breadcrumbs

2 tbsp pomegranate molasses

2 tsp ground cumin

salt and pepper

juice of 1 lemon

a small bunch of cilantro, roughly chopped

1 Halve and deseed the peppers and chili. Put the sweet peppers in an ovenproof dish, drizzle with a little of the olive oil and roast in an oven preheated to 375°F for 20 minutes. Add the chili to the peppers to roast for a further 10 minutes, or until they become soft.

2 Toast the walnuts in a dry pan on top of the stove, then put everything, except the remaining olive oil, lemon juice, and cilantro into a food processor. Add the sweet roasting juices from the peppers in the bottom of the pan, too.

3 Whizz all the ingredients together while adding the olive oil in a steady stream, then add half the lemon juice. Taste and season the mixture and add more lemon juice to taste.

4 Pour into a bowl, scatter with the chopped cilantro, and drizzle with extra-virgin olive oil.

DATE-STUFFED MACKEREL WITH SPICY BROTH AND COUSCOUS

Shad stuffed with dates is one of the great dishes of Moroccan cookery, though it's fiddly — the stoned dates are stuffed with rice, chopped almonds, and spices, and then used to stuff the fish. This is a simplified version, in which I've used mackerel instead of the much bonier shad, and added a broth. It's fantastically exotic — deep, dark, and spicy.

serves 4

4 x 6oz mackerel, scaled
    and gutted
olive oil
salt and pepper
½ tsp each of ground ginger
    and cinnamon
1¼ cups (10fl oz) fish stock
¼ tsp cayenne pepper
¼ tsp saffron threads
a small bunch of cilantro

FOR THE STUFFING
½ onion, finely chopped
1 tbsp olive oil
10 moist dates
¾ oz blanched almonds, toasted
3 tbsp mint leaves, chopped
finely grated rind and juice
    of ½ lemon
½ tsp ground ginger
¼ tsp *harissa* (*see* p19)
1oz butter

FOR THE COUSCOUS
7oz couscous
¾ cup (6fl oz) water
1 tbsp olive oil

1 For the stuffing, gently sauté the onion in the oil in a small pan until translucent. Tip into a bowl and leave to cool. Pit and roughly chop the dates. Crush the almonds so that you have a mixture of chunks and powdery pieces. Add the dates and almonds to the onion with all the other stuffing ingredients, including some salt and pepper, except for the butter. Dice the butter and, with your hands, mix it into the stuffing, then bring everything together into a ball.

2 Wash the mackerel thoroughly, cleaning away any bloody parts, which would make the fish taste bitter. With a sharp knife, gently open out the tail end a little, cutting along the inside of the fish beside the backbone — this is to give you a bigger pocket for stuffing.

3 Pour a little olive oil into the bottom of an ovenproof dish. Season the inside of all the fish, fill them with the stuffing, and lay them in the dish. Drizzle a little oil on the outside of each fish, rub with the ginger and cinnamon, and season with salt and pepper. Roast in an oven preheated to 350°F for 20 minutes.

4 Prepare the couscous by putting it into a broad, flat container and adding half the water. Leave it to plump up for about 10 minutes, then fork it through to separate the grains, and add the rest of the water, the olive oil and some salt and pepper. Leave the couscous to absorb the rest of the liquid, then fork and finger the grains until they are as separate as possible. Steam the couscous for 10 minutes. You can either use a steamer or a sieve lined with a clean dishcloth set over a pan of simmering water and covered.

5 Bring the stock to the boil and add the cayenne. Steep the saffron in a little boiled water and add it to the broth as well, together with salt and pepper if you think it needs it.

6 Roughly chop the cilantro. Get out your biggest, flattest soup bowls and put some couscous and 2 ladlefuls of broth in each one. Top with the mackerel and a handful of chopped cilantro.

FENNEL, POMEGRANATE, AND FETA SALAD

Salty and aniseedy with bursts of sour sweetness, this is a real palate cleanser.

serves 4

2 fennel bulbs

½ large cucumber

½ red onion, very finely sliced

a small bunch each of flat-leaf
 parsley and cilantro

7oz feta cheese

seeds of ½ pomegranate

FOR THE DRESSING

1½ tsp white-wine vinegar

2 tbsp extra-virgin olive oil

a pinch of superfine sugar

salt and pepper

1 Make the dressing by mixing together the vinegar, oil, sugar, salt, and pepper in the bottom of a shallow serving bowl.

2 Trim the fennel bulbs, reserving the little feathery fronds, and remove any tough outer leaves. Quarter the bulbs and cut out and discard the central core. Finely slice the fennel lengthwise, and toss it and the reserved fronds into the bowl containing the dressing.

3 Peel the cucumber and cut it in half lengthwise. Scoop out the central seeds with a teaspoon and slice the remaining flesh into half-moon shapes. Add to the bowl with the onion. Roughly chop the herbs and crumble the feta cheese and add them, too.

4 Toss the salad and scatter the pomegranate seeds on top – don't add the seeds before tossing, or they will leach out their crimson juices.

PROVENÇAL ROAST LAMB STUFFED WITH FIGS, GOAT CHEESE, AND WALNUTS

There's something gloriously decadent about using fresh figs in a stuffing, but you can use dried figs, soaked and chopped, with rather different results.

serves 6

1 x 4lb (boned weight) leg
 of lamb

salt and pepper

FOR THE STUFFING

½ tbsp olive oil

½ large onion, finely chopped

2¾oz walnut pieces

2¼oz breadcrumbs

5½oz goat cheese

8 fresh figs, quartered

leaves from 3 sprigs thyme

1 egg, beaten

1 Trim the lamb of any scraggy bits of fat, open it out flat and then season the inside.

2 Heat the oil in a sauté pan and cook the onion until soft. Toast the walnut pieces in a dry pan until just turning brown. Break the goat cheese into little nuggets. Gently mix all the stuffing ingredients together, bind with the egg, and season with salt and pepper. Spread the stuffing on the opened piece of lamb, roll it up, and tie at intervals with string.

3 Season the outside of the lamb and roast in an oven preheated to 400°F for 15 minutes, then turn the heat down to 375°F and cook for another hour – the lamb will be pink.

STUFFED FIGS DIPPED IN CHOCOLATE

Every pasticceria on the Amalfi coast seems to sell these — they're great with a bitter, dark espresso. I'm not one for messing around with petits fours, but these don't take much effort and I usually serve them instead of, rather than after, a dessert.

makes 40

40 dried, no-soak figs

40-60 unblanched almonds

1lb dark chocolate, no less
   than 70% cocoa solids

FOR THE MARZIPAN

5½ oz superfine sugar

5 tbsp water

5½ oz ground almonds, freshly
   ground if possible

juice and finely grated rind of
   ½ lemon

confectioner's sugar
   for dusting

1 For the marzipan, melt the sugar in the water over a low heat. When the sugar has dissolved, bring the liquid to boiling point and boil until the syrup has reached the "soft-ball" stage. Test for this by dropping a bit of the syrup into a glass of cold water; if it forms a little lump, it is at the right stage.

2 Now, working quickly, add the syrup to the almonds with the lemon juice and rind. Mix well. Use a wooden spoon to form it into a ball, then plonk it on your work surface. Using confectioner's sugar as you would use flour with pastry, knead the ball until it is lump-free. Wrap it loosely in foil and set aside to cool.

3 Make a little incision in the bottom of each fig to form a small hole. Stuff each fig with a chunk of marzipan and one or two whole almonds. When they're ready for coating, melt the chocolate in a bowl over a pan of simmering water. Dip each fig in the chocolate, coating it well, and then place on a sheet of waxed paper. Leave to set.

SPICED QUINCES WITH CREMA CATALANA ICE CREAM

Crema catalana ice cream is one of the dishes of modern Catalan cooking and a great spin on the classic crema catalana, basically a Catalan crème brûlée. It's now legion in this part of Spain and further afield (I first ate it in Cornwall).

serves 4

1¾ cups (14fl oz) white or
  red wine

4½ oz superfine sugar

1 sprig rosemary

½ cinnamon stick

1 bay leaf

2 large quinces

FOR THE ICE CREAM

2½ cups (20fl oz) whipping
  cream

⅞ cup (7fl oz) milk

1 cinnamon stick

2 strips lemon rind, white pith
  removed

4 egg yolks

10oz superfine sugar

1 Pour the wine into a saucepan and add the sugar, rosemary, cinnamon stick, and bay leaf. Heat gently until the sugar has dissolved.

2 Peel the quinces, cut them in half, and core. Put them in the warm wine, bring to the boil, and then simmer until they are tender, turning them over every so often. It could take as long as 45 minutes before they get soft.

3 Remove the herbs and cinnamon. You should find that the poaching liquid is quite syrupy – there's so much pectin in quinces – and it will thicken more as it cools. If it does seem a bit thin, remove the quinces and boil the syrup to reduce it a little, then put the quinces back and leave everything to cool.

4 To make the ice cream, heat the cream and the milk with the cinnamon stick and lemon rind to just below boiling. Remove from the heat and leave to infuse for half an hour. Beat the egg yolks with 4½ oz of the sugar until smooth and creamy in color. Bring the cream and milk to just below boiling point again and then slowly strain it through a sieve over the beaten yolks and sugar, stirring as you do so. In a bowl set over a pan of simmering water, heat this until it thickens enough to coat the back of a spoon.

5 Quickly pour the custard into a clean bowl sitting in a sink of cold water. Let it cool and then chill in the refrigerator.

6 Make the caramel by melting the rest of the sugar with 4 tbsp water. Heat gently until the sugar has dissolved, then boil hard until the sugar goes from pale gold to caramel-colored. Immediately pour this onto a lightly greased baking sheet. Leave it to get hard and then break it up by bashing it in a plastic bag with a rolling pin. You want to end up with small shards.

7 Freeze the custard – either in your freezer, giving it a good beating every so often to break up the crystals, or in an ice-cream machine – incorporating the caramel chips towards the end of freezing so that they don't get broken down.

8 Give each person half a quince with its syrup and a couple of scoops of ice cream alongside.

"...The quinces, never to be outgrown in affection, would hang like yellow lanterns on the trees after the leaves had fallen, the most lasting of the orchard's beauty and none more appetizing stewed or baked or in pies with clotted cream or preserved in jellies and jams"

MILES FRANKLIN, *CHILDHOOD AT BRINDABELLA*

FIG AND BARBERRY ICE CREAM

I once saw this on the menu of a Persian restaurant, but they had run out by the time I came to order dessert. It sounded such a steeped-in-the-fabled-East kind of a dish that I had to come home and try it out for myself. The tartness of the barberries is perfect as a counterfoil to the richness of the figs.

serves 6-8

1lb fresh figs

3 tbsp water

1 tbsp cassis

1oz dried barberries

a good squeeze of lemon juice

3 egg yolks

3½oz superfine sugar

1¾ cups (14fl oz)
   whipping cream

1 Snip the stem ends off the figs and quarter them. Put them in a saucepan with the water, cover, and stew gently for about 15 minutes until very soft. Purée in the food processor and add the cassis, barberries, and lemon juice. Leave to cool.

2 Beat the egg yolks with the sugar until creamy. Heat the whipping cream until just below boiling point, then slowly pour it over the sugar and yolk mixture, stirring as you do so. Set this bowl over a pan of simmering water and cook, stirring continually, until the mixture thickens. Do not let it heat so much that it scrambles – go gently and patiently. Check the consistency of the custard by coating the back of your spoon with it. Glide your finger through this; if it leaves a clear channel, then the mixture is thick enough. Pour the custard into a bowl and let it cool.

3 Chill both the custard and the fruit purée, then mix them together. Either freeze in an ice cream machine, or still-freeze, beating the mixture every so often during the freezing process.

CARDAMOM-BAKED FIGS AND PLUMS WITH BURNT HONEY AND YOGURT PANNACOTTA

I first made this to get rid of a load of figs and plums which were past their best — it's a great throw-it-all-together-and-slam-it-in-the-oven kind of dish. If you don't feel like making the pannacotta, just do the baked fruit and serve Greek yogurt, drizzled with a little honey, on the side. That's how I do it nine times out of ten, but sometimes it's nice to be fancy.

serves 4

FOR THE FRUIT

8 figs

6 plums

zest of 1 lime

juice of 2 limes

seeds from 4 cardamom
   pods, crushed

½ cup (4fl oz) orange juice

¼ cup (2fl oz) water

3oz soft dark brown sugar

FOR THE PANNACOTTA

5 tbsp clear honey

3 tbsp orange juice

2½ gelatine leaves

⅝ cup (5fl oz) heavy cream

1¾ cups (14fl oz) Greek yogurt

groundnut (peanut) oil,
   for greasing

1 Halve the figs and halve and stone the plums. Put them in a shallow ovenproof dish and add all the other ingredients for the fruit, sprinkling finally with the brown sugar — make sure that some of it stays on top of the fruit, where it will caramelize. Put the dish in an oven preheated to 350°F for 20-25 minutes. The fruit should be soft and slightly browned. You can serve it lukewarm, but I love it chilled.

2 To make the pannacotta, put the honey in a small saucepan and bring to the boil. The honey will eventually caramelise — it will go darker, but it is the caramelized smell that will tell you when it's ready. Immediately take the pan off the heat and add the orange juice. Put the pan back over the heat for just long enough to melt the honey again and incorporate the juice. Let this cool completely.

3 Put the gelatine into enough cold water to cover. Let it soak for about 10 minutes. Meanwhile, heat half of the heavy cream. Squeeze all the water out of the softened gelatine and add the gelatine to the warm cream. Stir to dissolve and let the cream cool, but don't let it go absolutely cold or the gelatine will start to set it.

4 Stir the cream and gelatine mixture into the yogurt. Add the rest of the cream and the honey. Lightly grease four *bavarois* molds (or small teacups, anything that will work as a little mould) with some groundnut (peanut) oil. Divide the yogurt mixture among the molds and refrigerate. They'll take about 3 hours to set.

5 Unmold a pannacotta onto each plate — I usually just loosen around the edges with a fish fileting knife then invert it on the plate, giving it a good shake. You may find you need to set the molds in some very hot water just for a second to help. Serve with the figs and plums alongside.

CURDS AND WHEY

YOGURT, FETA, AND RICOTTA

I used to loathe yogurt. When I was growing up, the refrigerator was always full of those sour-yet-sickly-sweet little pots of the stuff that hadn't so much as sniffed a strawberry. My sister, who claimed that eating was boring, could always be prevailed upon to eat one of these in lieu of a proper meal, thus confirming my suspicions that this thin, acidic gloop was fit only for people who didn't like food.

Then, as an *au-pair* in France, I discovered set natural yogurt. It came in a blue-and-white carton of minimalist design. *Yaourt Nature* had a milky film on top and trembled like a blancmange when you sliced your spoon through it. I was shown how to sprinkle soft, dark-brown sugar on the yogurt's surface and let it melt, making a burnt-toffee-tasting crust, a sweet piece of which was to be incorporated into every sour mouthful. My taste buds went wild at the onslaught, and I can honestly say that I would still prefer to eat this than the most perfectly made crème brûlée.

Soon after that, I discovered the luscious Greek stuff. I had made a jar of "Greek marmalade", a blissful confection of chopped nuts and dried apricots mixed with warm honey and mint, and thought it deserved something better than toast. With Greek yogurt, it made one of those desserts whose virtue belies its deliciousness. I couldn't believe that something this rich wasn't as high in fat as heavy cream (Greek yogurt has a fifth of heavy cream's fat content). I'd never liked the airy sweetness of whipped cream anyway, so I embraced this yogurt's tartness, its texture — as creamy as a classy moisturizer — and the way it fell in great thick folds. Greek yogurt made with cows milk is less tart and more creamy than the ewes-milk version, but both are thick because they have already been partially drained. I always serve this yogurt, mixed with a little pouring cream and sweetened with confectioner's sugar and vanilla extract, with desserts. The sourness provides the perfect antidote to sugary meringues and sticky toffee pudding and makes an x-rated dessert out of berries and bittersweet chocolate cake. It produces a clean, fresh-tasting ice cream; a nice, tart pannacotta to go with poached or baked fruit; and, added to custard, a fuller, more balanced base than plain cream for fruit fools.

You won't find little pots of commercial sweetened yogurt in refrigerators in the Middle East, but big basins of sour, creamy stuff. There, it's as basic a necessity as bread, and is used in savory dishes more than sweet ones. Yogurt's a sauce, dip, cooking medium, and tenderizer. With a little crushed garlic, it makes a moist, soothing cooler that goes well with the musky sweetness of spices and big, fat flavors such as chili. Dishes of stewed lentils with cumin, lamb pilafs dotted with almonds and apricots and smoky grilled eggplants... they all love the starkness of yogurt.

In Iran, where yogurt is particularly popular (it was originally referred to as "Persian milk" in parts of the Middle East), yogurt dishes even have their own collective name: *boorani* (after Queen Poorandokht, who loved yogurt so much that the royal chefs kept trying out new dishes with it). Such cooling Iranian offerings as spinach and garlic with yogurt, or fried eggplant with yogurt, were invented to please the royal palate.

The Turks' *yogurtlu* dishes use yogurt as a layering ingredient, spreading it over beds of torn pita to be topped with braised lamb and tomatoes, or sandwiching it between rags of flatbread, salad, and hot broiled lamb. The mix of temperatures and textures is delicious. I also love the crusty, creamy blanket formed when yogurt is mixed with eggs and cheese and baked. The Greeks pour this tart custard over dishes of lamb and vegetables or chicken joints before baking. These make brilliant supper dishes – the best kind of home cooking. Just remember that you need to stabilize the yogurt, which would otherwise split when heated, by adding a little salt and 1 tablespoon of cornstarch (mixed to a paste with a little cold water) per 1¾ pints of yogurt.

It might seem excessive to make your own yogurt cheese, or *labneh*, but it's the easiest thing in the world. It simply entails putting thick Greek yogurt into a square of muslin, tying it at the top, and hanging it up or setting it in a sieve so that the whey can run off into a basin or the sink. Even after an hour the yogurt will have thickened substantially, but I generally leave it for twenty-four hours. I like the sound of the still, slow dripping as something else is formed. It's somehow primeval, and the nearest I will ever get to the earthy business of cheese-making. It reminds me that milk is a living thing. Unwrapping the yogurt, you find a firm cushion imprinted with the texture of the muslin. It always seems such a pity to break this up, but I do. I put little cold nuggets of it among spicy roast vegetables, or mix it with crushed garlic and a little salt to make a spread for bread. Drained yogurt's particularly good with sweet things, such as slow roast tomatoes and onions. Or form it into little balls, roll these in paprika or chopped herbs, and then put them in a jar and cover with olive oil; perfect for *mezze*.

You can also slice your drained yogurt into thick, cake-type wedges, leaving the muslin pattern intact, and drizzle it with honey or a honey and flower water syrup. Serve this with sliced fruit: peaches, mangoes or oranges. Healthy but gorgeous.

I use the more runny type of natural yogurt for marinades. Its higher acidity makes it a more effective tenderizer and its liquidity allows it to penetrate the incisions in chicken or lamb. But apart from this, as far as yogurt goes, Greece is the word.

Cheese is almost as important as yogurt in the Middle East and Eastern Europe. The Greeks actually eat more cheese per head than the French every year, hardly surprising when you think it's popular even for breakfast. Apart from *labneh*, feta-type cheeses (the Turkish version is called *beyaz peynir*) are the most popular and certainly the simplest to make. Once the curds have formed, the whey is drained off and the curds are pressed. When they're firm enough, the curds are salted and left to dry for twenty-four hours before being steeped in brine. After only a month it's ready to eat and is sold in the manner that gives it its name – *feta* is the Greek word for "slice".

Unfortunately the feta available in supermarkets gives you no clue as to how good it can be. In Greece, feta is usually made with unpasteurized sheep or goats milk, elsewhere it can be made with pasteurized cows milk, producing a cheese that doesn't taste of much except for salt. Although the best examples still have this characteristic saltiness, they vary widely in pungency and crumbliness. Turkish *beyaz peynir* is usually made with cows milk, but it, too, varies a lot, and non-factory-made versions are always better. If you can, buy your feta or *beyaz peynir* from a Greek or Turkish deli.

Outside Greece and Turkey people don't get particularly excited about feta-type cheese, but I love it. Like yogurt cheese, it goes well with sweet things – its tangy crumbs are a delicious contrast to roast pumpkin, sweet potatoes, and roast peppers. Conversely, its sharpness is good with the fresh greenness of cucumber and herbs such as mint, dill, and tarragon. Mixed with eggs, herbs, and perhaps the sharper *kefalotyri* (a hard Greek cheese that is a bit like Italian pecorino), feta can make endless fillings for Greek filo pies – just add leeks or spinach, pumpkin or chicken, zucchini or eggplant, and spoon it into a case of buttered filo leaves. I must say that I also like feta for its texture – it's very satisfying to crumble handfuls of it over a simple Greek lamb and tomato stew; no grating or shaving or any of that malarky, just a bowl of those little tiny pasta shapes called orzo, and you're done.

I always think ricotta is like a baby cheese – it smells sweetly milky and tastes so mild. It's also unformed: its grainy curds separating when you dig your fork into it. But then, ricotta's hardly a cheese at all; it's a by-product of cheese-making. Milk is added to the whey that is left over from other cheeses. A little sour whey or some other coagulant is added and the whole thing is heated (hence the name *ricotta* or "re-cooked") until lumps of ricotta form on the surface. Fresh ricotta is creamy white, delicately crumbly and bears as much relation to those plastic tubs of supermarket stuff as thick Jersey cream does to Cool Whip. Until you've tasted good ricotta, the point of simple dishes such as pasta with fried zucchini, ricotta, and basil will elude you.

The Sicilians, who are often credited with inventing ricotta, adore it, although I can pass on their specialty, *cassata*. It's an overly sweet, baroque fantasy of a cake – layers of cake, sweetened ricotta, and candied fruit topped with pistachio-colored marzipan – I'd love to like it, but can't. However, I will mix ricotta with cream and eggs, bitter chocolate, and grated orange or booze-soaked raisins for a tart filling. Or I'll blend sweetened ricotta and thick cream with lemon zest and juice to fill a sponge. In fact, ricotta is a "filler" *par excellence*, partly because it's such a good carrier of flavors: spinach, nuts, Parmesan, delicate herbs, nutmeg, and flower waters – it perfectly transmits all their nuances.

There are even simpler pleasures though. Italians make a kind of deconstructed tiramisu by mashing coffee and sugar into ricotta and serving it with cake fingers. I've often served a bowl of fresh ricotta with dark, sweet cherries. And for a snack, ricotta's good on warm ciabatta sprinkled with olive oil and basil leaves. The best thing about yogurt, feta, and ricotta is their purity, their simple, clean flavors. They're enjoyable without undergoing any cooking. I'll happily breakfast on bread spread with drained yogurt and honey; I'll snack on a wedge of feta with olives and herbs; I'll have a lunch of ricotta with warm, oil-sprinkled spring vegetables, or finish a meal with a mound of ricotta mashed with crushed raspberries and sugar. With ingredients this good, you can eat well without cooking.

BULGAR AND SPINACH PILAF WITH LABNEH AND CHILI ROAST TOMATOES

This Turkish dish has layers of flavor and texture: nutty bulgar wheat; hot, sweet tomatoes; chunks of cool labneh; and cinnamon onions. It is great with lamb or as a vegetarian main course.

serves 4 as a main course,
8 as a side dish

1 onion, finely chopped

4 tbsp olive oil

2 garlic cloves, crushed

6oz bulgar wheat

1¼ cups (10fl oz) chicken or
    vegetable stock

salt and pepper

10½oz spinach

leaves from a small bunch of
    mint, torn

extra-virgin olive oil

FOR THE LABNEH

1⅛ cups (9fl oz) Greek yogurt

1 fat garlic clove, crushed

pinch of salt

FOR THE TOMATOES

12 plum tomatoes

4 tbsp olive oil

2 tbsp balsamic vinegar

1-1½ tsp *harissa* (*see* p19)

2tsp) soft dark-brown
sugar

FOR THE ONIONS

2 onions, very finely sliced

2 tbsp olive oil

½ tsp ground cinnamon

1½ tsp soft brown sugar

juice of ½ small lemon

1 Make the *labneh* according to the recipe on p139, seasoning it with a little salt.

2 Halve the tomatoes lengthwise and put them in a small roasting pan or ovenproof dish. Mix together the olive oil, balsamic vinegar, *harissa*, and some salt and pepper, and pour this over the tomatoes. Turn them over, making sure they get coated, ending with them cut-side up. Sprinkle the soft brown sugar over the top and put in an oven preheated to 350°F. Cook for 40-45 minutes, until the tomatoes are shrunken and sweet. They can either be hot or at room temperature when you add them to the pilaf, so you could do this part in advance.

3 For the pilaf, sauté the chopped onion in half the olive oil in a fairly heavy-bottomed saucepan. When the onion is soft and translucent, add the garlic and cook for another couple of minutes. Tip the bulgar wheat into the pan, pour in the stock, and season. Bring to the boil, then turn down the heat and let the bulgar simmer in the stock for about 15 minutes. All the stock will have been absorbed by then. Cover the pot and let the bulgar sit to fluff up for another 10 minutes.

4 Take the stalks off the spinach and wash the leaves well. In a covered pot, cook the leaves in just the water that clings to them after washing. They will wilt in about 4 minutes. Squeeze out the excess moisture and chop the leaves very roughly. Sauté the spinach for a few minutes in the remaining olive oil and season it well with salt and pepper. Stir this into the bulgar wheat.

5 Quickly cook the finely sliced onions in very hot olive oil – you want them golden brown with some crispy bits. For the last minute of cooking time, add the cinnamon and brown sugar. Stir this around and, once the sugar has melted and begun to slightly caramelize, add a good squeeze of lemon juice and some salt and pepper.

6 Layer the different components in a broad, shallow bowl: tip in the bulgar wheat, sprinkle on half the mint, then the tomatoes, then the rest of the mint. Break the *labneh* into lumps and scatter them over the tomatoes. Now strew the onions on top, drizzle with a slug of extra-virgin olive oil, and serve.

YOGURT MEZZE

Yogurt makes a great basis for the little dishes known as mezze *which are served all over the Middle East. Add garlic and herbs, grated or chopped cucumber, sliced radish, little cubes of cooked eggplant, nuts or dried fruit for a range of textures and flavors that are used from Georgia to Egypt. And don't just serve them as* mezze *— they're all great counterparts to dishes of spiced roast lamb, grilled chicken or pilaf. Make those containing cucumber no more than 2 hours before you want to serve them, or the water in the cucumber will leach out.*

FOR THE YOGURT BASE

1½ cups (12fl oz) Greek yogurt

1 garlic clove, crushed

salt and pepper

FOR THE RAISIN,

ALMOND, AND CUCUMBER

1½ oz raisins

1½ oz blanched almonds

½ cucumber

a small handful of cilantro

2 tsp *harissa* (*see* p19)

2 tbsp olive oil

FOR THE CHERRY,

WALNUT, AND DILL

2oz dried sour cherries

1½ oz shelled walnuts

½ cucumber

2 tbsp dill, chopped

a little sumac, optional

FOR THE POMEGRANATE,

WALNUT, MINT, AND ROSE

1½ oz shelled walnuts

seeds from 2 pomegranates

a small handful of

   mint, chopped

¼ tsp rose water

a few edible rose petals or

   pomegranate seeds to serve

To make enough yogurt base for one of the following *mezze*, simply mix all the base ingredients together. Then add the other ingredients.

RAISIN, ALMOND, AND CUCUMBER

Soak the raisins in hot water for 15 minutes until they plump up. Toast the almonds in a dry frying pan then chop them very roughly. Halve the cucumber lengthwise, scoop out and discard the seedy center using a small spoon, and cut the flesh into cubes. Mix the drained raisins with all the other ingredients and the yogurt base, taste for seasoning, and serve.

SOUR CHERRY, WALNUT, AND DILL

Soak the cherries in hot water and prepare the nuts and cucumber as in the previous recipe. Drain the cherries and mix with the nuts, cucumber, and dill into the yogurt base. Check for seasoning and sprinkle a little sumac (a crimson-colored, citrus-fruit-tasting spice) on top.

POMEGRANATE, WALNUT, MINT, AND ROSE

Toast the nuts in a dry pan, chop them roughly and mix them together with all the other ingredients, stirring gently so as not to break up the yogurt base and the pomegranate seeds. Check for seasoning and garnish with a few rose petals, torn or shredded, or a handful of pomegranate seeds if you prefer.

SAVORY AND SWEET FRITELLE DI RICOTTA

Ah, ricotta fritters – you always intend to make them but wimp out in case they fall apart and you faint from the trauma of deep-frying. Fear not – these work.

SAVORY FRITTERS

serves 4 as a lunch with salad, 8 as an appetizer

1lb 2oz spinach

9oz ricotta cheese

a good 1oz all-purpose flour

2¾oz Parmesan, grated

1 egg plus 2 egg yolks

freshly grated nutmeg

salt and pepper

groundnut oil for deep-frying

flour for dusting

1 De-stalk and wash the spinach and cook it in the water that clings to it. It will take about 4 minutes in a covered saucepan over a medium heat.

2 Drain the spinach well, then squeeze out the excess moisture. Put it together with all the other ingredients, apart from the oil, and mix in a food processor using the pulse button (or chop the spinach and mix everything by hand if you prefer). Taste and adjust the seasoning.

3 Lightly flour your hands and form the mixture into little dumplings – just a little smaller than golf balls. Slightly flatten them and put them on floured baking sheets or plates. Chill these well in the refrigerator.

4 Cook the fritters at the last minute, deep-frying them in about 6¼ inches of hot oil until they are a deep, golden brown. The oil has to be hot (or the fritters will fall apart), but not too hot (or they will burn on the outside before they are hot in the middle). The recipe gives you enough mixture to have a few disasters before you get the oil to the optimum temperature.

5 Drain the fritters on absorbent paper towels and serve immediately.

SWEET FRITTERS

serves 4

8oz ricotta cheese

2 eggs, beaten

a good 1oz unsalted butter

1½oz superfine sugar

a good 1oz all-purpose flour

finely grated rind of 1 orange

½ tsp vanilla extract

groundnut oil for frying

confectioner's sugar
  for dusting

FOR THE SYRUP

juice of 3 oranges and
  2 lemons

2¼oz superfine sugar

1 To make the syrup, simply mix the juices and sugar together in a saucepan and heat gently, stirring from time to time to help the sugar melt. Bring to the boil and boil for about 10 minutes, until reduced and syrupy. Set this aside to cool, then put it into a jug and chill.

2 Mash the ricotta, adding the eggs bit by bit. Melt the butter and add it to the ricotta with all the other ingredients apart from the oil and dusting sugar. Mix to a smooth batter.

3 Heat about 1½ inches of oil in a frying pan. Spoon the batter into the oil, about 1 tbsp per fritter. You should be able to cook about five at once. Cook until browned on one side, then turn them over and cook on the other side. They are so light they cook in about 4 minutes.

4 Drain the fritters on paper towels, pile them on to a plate, sift confectioner's sugar over the top, and serve immediately with the syrup.

BAKED SWEET POTATOES WITH MARINATED FETA AND BLACK OLIVES

Sweet potatoes are not everyday fare in the Mediterranean, so this is not a traditional dish, but the combination of sweet, warm flesh and cold, salty olives and feta is irresistible. Roast pumpkin works well, too.

serves 4

4 medium sweet potatoes

a little olive oil

black pepper

4½ oz black kalamata olives

a small bunch of cilantro,
    roughly chopped

FOR THE FETA

7oz feta cheese, roughly
    broken up

½ tbsp fennel seeds

1 medium red chili, deseeded
    and cut into fine slivers

1 garlic clove, crushed

½ tsp coriander seeds, crushed

extra-virgin olive oil

1 Mix the feta with the other ingredients and just enough oil to moisten it. Cover and set in a cool place or refrigerate to allow the flavors to meld.

2 Bake the sweet potatoes in their skins in an oven preheated to 350°F. They should be just tender, which will take about 50 minutes, but do check with a skewer – it really depends upon the size of your potatoes.

3 When the potatoes are cooked, split them open lengthwise, like you would a baked potato. Sprinkle with a little oil and freshly ground black pepper, and fill with the marinated feta. Divide the olives and cilantro among the four potatoes and serve.

"Next he sat down to milk his ewes and his bleating goats, which he did methodically, putting the young to each mother as he finished. He then curdled half the white milk, collected the whey, and stored it in wicker cheesebaskets…"

HOMER, *THE ODYSSEY*

OTTOMAN LAMB WITH SULTAN'S PLEASURE

This is based on a recipe in the late Jeremy Round's brilliant book The Independent Cook *(now, happily, back in print). I've been cooking this lamb for years and have changed it only slightly. The eggplant purée, the part of the dish that is the 'Sultan's Pleasure', is actually a traditional dish, usually served with braised lamb and tomatoes. According to legend, it was rustled up by a resourceful cook to feed a sultan who got lost in the forest. Needless to say, he liked it.*

serves 4-6

1 x 4lb leg of lamb

FOR THE MARINADE

⅞ cup (7fl oz) plain yogurt

2 tbsp tomato purée

4 tbsp red wine

4 tbsp olive oil

4 garlic cloves, crushed

3 bay leaves, crushed

1 tsp superfine sugar

1 tsp salt

½ tsp black pepper

1 tsp cayenne pepper

FOR THE PURÉE

1½ lb eggplant

olive oil

1½ oz butter

1½ oz all-purpose flour

275ml (9½fl oz) whole milk

1oz Parmesan, grated

2oz feta cheese, crumbled

salt and pepper

TO SERVE

watercress or fresh cilantro

extra-virgin olive oil

cayenne pepper

1 Remove the skin and fat from the lamb, exposing as much flesh as possible. Make incisions all over the leg with a small, sharp knife. Mix the marinade ingredients together and pour over the lamb, rubbing it into the incisions. Leave the lamb to marinate for 24 hours if you can, and for at least an hour if you can't.

2 To make the Sultan's Pleasure, drizzle the whole eggplants with a little olive oil and roast them for half an hour in an oven preheated to 350°F. Remove from the oven and leave them to cool.

3 Slit the eggplants and scoop out the pulp inside. Press the mixture in a sieve with the back of a spoon to get rid of some of the juices. Purée.

4 Drain the lamb from its marinade but don't wipe it clean. Roast it for 1¼ hours at 375°F (this will give you pink lamb), then cover it with foil and insulate it (I keep a pile of old towels for this) to keep it warm. Leave it for 15 minutes to let the juices set.

5 Make a white sauce by melting the butter and adding the flour. Stir the flour over a low heat until it forms a roux and goes pale gold in color. Take this off the heat and add the milk, slowly at first, making sure the liquid is well-amalgamated before you add the rest. Put this back on the heat and bring to boiling point, stirring all the time, until the sauce is thick. Let this simmer for about 5 minutes. Add the eggplant purée and cheeses to the sauce. Stir, taste, and season with salt and pepper.

6 Serve the lamb on a platter with some sprigs of very fresh cilantro or watercress round the bone end, and a mound of the purée at the other. Drizzle the purée with a little extra-virgin olive oil and sprinkle with a bit of cayenne. Alternatively, carve the lamb and serve the slices on a bed of the purée scattered with some chopped fresh cilantro.

ROAST VEGETABLES WITH LABNEH AND ZHUG

This dish is a really good layering of hot spices, sweet vegetables and the cool, cool soothingness of yogurt cheese. Zhug is a chili and cardamom sauce from the Yemen, now very popular in Israel as well. You can use it as a dip, a sauce, or, mixed with more olive oil and lime, as a marinade for chicken or lamb. Be careful with it, though — it really does bite!

serves 4

2 red peppers

1 large eggplant

8 plum tomatoes

1 red onion

6 tbsp olive oil

salt and pepper

FOR THE LABNEH

1¾ cups (14fl oz) Greek yogurt

2 garlic cloves, crushed

salt and pepper

FOR THE *ZHUG*

3 medium green chilies

2 red bird's-eye chilies

seeds from 8 cardamom pods

1½ tsp caraway seeds

3 garlic cloves

a large bunch of cilantro

½ cup (4fl oz) extra-virgin
    olive oil

a good squeeze of fresh lime
    juice, or to taste

1 You have to start the *labneh* the day before. Just line a sieve with a bit of cheesecloth and set it over a small bowl. Put the yogurt into the cheesecloth and refrigerate the whole thing. The yogurt will lose a bit of excess moisture over the next 24 hours, leaving you with a firmer mixture, a bit like cream cheese. Help it by giving it a bit of a squeeze once or twice.

2 Tumble the drained yogurt into a bowl. Add the garlic, a little salt and pepper, and mash it all together. Cover and put the *labneh* in the refrigerator until you need it.

3 Halve and deseed the peppers and cut each half lengthwise into four broad strips. Cut the eggplant into rounds, quarter the largest slices, and halve the rest. Halve the tomatoes and the onion and cut the onion into half-moon-shaped slices.

4 Put all the vegetables into a roasting pan with the olive oil and seasoning. Gently turn the vegetables over to coat them in the oil, then roast them in an oven preheated to 375°F for 40 minutes.

5 To make the *zhug*, halve and deseed the chilies — be careful not to rub your eyes with your hands afterwards, as the bird's-eyes in particular are very strong — and put them into a food processor with the spices, garlic, and cilantro. Add the olive oil with the motor running. Taste and add a really good squeeze of lime — I generally end up using half a lime, but see what you like. Add some salt to taste as well.

6 Break the *labneh* up into smallish chunks and dot it among the vegetables. Spoon some of the *zhug* over the top and put the rest into a bowl so that people can help themselves. Serve with warm Arab bread or ciabatta.

CHICKEN MARINATED IN YOGURT WITH GEORGIAN PLUM SAUCE

The plum accompaniment is my version of the Georgian classic, tkemali, *a thick, sweet, dark crimson sauce which, supposedly, separates good Georgian cooks from great ones. Georgia is not on the Mediterranean coast, but it uses so many of the ingredients we associate with Turkey — pomegranates, lemons, garlic, walnuts, yogurt, feta, dill, and mint — and its cooking is so Mediterranean in spirit, that I couldn't resist including it.*

Some cooks make the sauce only with plums, leaving out the prunes, so do it like that if you prefer. In Georgia this is a celebrated accompaniment to tabaka *(flattened fried chicken) and is even stirred into hot kidney beans to make a* mezze. *Try it with grilled mackerel or lamb kebabs. It is fine in the refrigerator for a month.*

serves 4

1⅛ cups (9fl oz) plain yogurt
(ordinary plain, not Greek)

4 garlic cloves, crushed

juice of ½ lemon

1 tsp ground cinnamon

½ tsp cayenne pepper

salt and pepper

8 chicken thighs, or a mixture
of leg and breast joints,
skin on

FOR THE PLUM SAUCE

14oz plums

3½ oz prunes

1½ oz dark, soft-brown sugar

1½ fl oz red-wine vinegar

1½ fl oz water

½ tsp cayenne pepper

2 garlic cloves, crushed

a large bunch of herbs (mix of
cilantro, dill, and mint),
roughly chopped

a squeeze of lemon
juice (optional)

1 Mix the yogurt, garlic, lemon juice, spices, and seasoning together to make a marinade. Put the chicken into this, covering it well, and leave it to marinate for 2 hours, or overnight if possible, turning it over a couple of times.

2 Halve the plums and prunes and remove the stones. Put all the ingredients for the plum sauce, except the herbs and lemon juice, into a saucepan and bring gently to the boil. Immediately turn down to a simmer and cook the plums for half an hour.

3 Purée the mixture and put it back into the saucepan. Add the herbs — keeping some back to sprinkle on top just before serving — and heat slightly just to bring the flavor of the herbs out. Check the seasoning; I don't usually add anything else but you may want some salt or the added freshness of a bit of lemon juice. Turn the sauce into a bowl and let it cool.

4 Take the chicken out of the marinade and grill it on each side, on a high heat at first, to get a good color. Then turn the heat down and let the chicken cook through.

5 Sprinkle a few chopped fresh herbs on to the plum sauce and serve it with the chicken. A bowl of Greek yogurt mixed with chopped cucumber and crushed garlic is really good with it, and provide flatbread or a dish of bulgar wheat.

"The Turks are no whit acquainted with fresh
butter, there being little, or none at all, made
about Constantinople; neither do they eat much
milk, except it be made sowre, which they call
yoghurd. For that, being so turned sowre, it
doth quench the thirst."

OTTAVIANO BON, *THE SULTAN'S SERAGLIO*

YOGURT AND WALNUT CAKE WITH COFFEE SYRUP

I wanted to include a yogurt cake – they are so easy, and I can never quite believe those white curds will turn into anything edible once they're mixed with flour – and also a walnut cake. They are both so redolent of Turkey and Greece. This, then, is a fusion of the two. In their homelands these cakes are usually served soaked in a thick, sugary syrup – too sweet even for me – so I've toned that down.

serves 8-10

6oz butter

6oz superfine sugar

2 eggs

¾ cup (6fl oz) plain yogurt

6oz shelled walnuts, 4½oz of
 which are roughly chopped,
 the remainder ground

6oz self-raising flour

1 tsp baking powder

confectioner's sugar for sifting

FOR THE SYRUP

1¼ cups (10fl oz) strong
 coffee (espresso)

3oz superfine sugar

2 tbsp brandy

1 Cream the butter and sugar together until light and fluffy. Add the eggs, one at a time, and continue to beat. Stir in the yogurt and the nuts.

2 Sift the flour and baking powder and fold them into the batter. Pour into a greased and lined eight-inch cake pan. Bake in an oven preheated to 350°F for 40 minutes, or until a skewer inserted into the middle comes out clean.

3 Mix the coffee with the sugar and boil to reduce by half. Add the brandy.

4 While the cake is still warm, pierce it all over with a skewer and pour the coffee syrup on to it. Leave the cake in its pan overnight.

5 Unmold the cake and dust it with confectioner's sugar. Serve it with plain Greek yogurt if you want to be really simple, or a mixture of mascarpone and a little fromage frais or low-fat cream cheese, into which you have stirred some brandy-based liqueur.

LOU CACHAT

A kind of Provençal cheese spread, generally made by fromagiers *from leftover bits of cheese. That might not sound too appetizing, but in fact this is worth making even if you don't have leftovers. In theory you can use any cheeses, but the following is a good combination. It's got real bite.*

serves 8 as a cheese course

3½ oz goat cheese

1oz Roquefort cheese

2½ tbsp crème fraîche
   or sour cream

1½ tbsp brandy or *eau de vie*

black pepper

1 Mash the cheeses together and add the crème fraîche or sour cream, brandy or *eau de vie*, and pepper. The mixture should be slightly chunky.

2 Serve on rounds of toasted baguette as a cheese course, or as part of an appetizer with *tapenade* or *anchoïade*, or just plain good olives and a bunch of radishes.

RICOTTA ICE CREAM WITH POMEGRANATE AND BLOOD-ORANGE SAUCE

Sicilians love ricotta ice cream, and nobody makes it better than master ice cream maker Corrado Constanzo, from Noto, whose recipe this is. Corrado, well into his seventies, lectured me on the evils of commercial ice cream, "pumped up with air", so your lowly domestic ice cream machine, or even your own hand mixing, is just right for this. The sauce, since it uses classic Sicilian fruits, is a perfect partner.

serves 4-6

1lb 2oz ricotta cheese

⅝ cup (5fl oz) milk

2¼ oz confectioner's sugar

⅝ cup (5fl oz) whipping cream

FOR THE SAUCE

juice of 1 pomegranate

¾ cup (6fl oz) fresh
   blood-orange juice

2 strips orange rind

3oz superfine sugar

seeds of 2 pomegranates

1 tbsp orange-flower water

1 Beat the ricotta to a cream and add the milk and sugar. Lightly whip the cream and stir it in. Either still-freeze, beating several times during the freezing process, or churn in an ice cream machine.

2 Put the juices, rind, and sugar into a small saucepan and heat gently, stirring until the sugar has dissolved. Boil for 5 minutes or until the liquid becomes slightly syrupy.

3 Let the syrup cool, then remove the orange rind. Add the pomegranate seeds and the orange-flower water and serve with the ice cream.

YOGURT, HONEY, AND PISTACHIO CHEESECAKE WITH ORANGES IN CARDAMOM SYRUP

This isn't a true cheesecake as it has no cheese in it! It's really more of a torte. I've made it with oatmeal cookies, nutty cookies, even ginger cookies, so choose whatever seems right for you.

serves 8

FOR THE COOKIE BASE

5½ oz sweet cookies

2oz blanched almonds

2¾ oz butter

FOR THE CREAM

2¼ cups (18fl oz) Greek yogurt

2¼ cups (18fl oz) crème
   fraîche or sour cream

8 tbsp orange- blossom honey

2 tsp orange-flower water

rind and juice of 1 orange

1 sachet powdered gelatine

FOR THE ORANGES

¾ cup (6fl oz) orange juice

juice of 1 lime

½ cup (4fl oz) water

8 tbsp clear honey

seeds from 8 cardamom
   pods, crushed

4 oranges

To serve

2¼ oz chopped pistachios

confectioner's sugar
   for dusting

1 For the cookie base, bash the cookies and nuts together in a plastic bag (make sure there are no holes in it) using a rolling pin. You want to end up with quite a textured mixture. Melt the butter and mix it with the ground nuts and cookies.

2 Lightly grease an eight-inch springform pan and line it with a disk of baking parchment. Press the cookie and butter mixture into this and put it in the refrigerator to firm up for an hour or so.

3 In a bowl, mix together the yogurt, crème fraîche or sour cream, honey, orange-flower water, and orange rind. Put the orange juice in a small heavy-bottomed saucepan and sprinkle over the powdered gelatine. Let it "sponge" for about 5 minutes then put it over a very low heat and gently melt it. Pour immediately over the yogurt mix, stirring as you do so. Pour this on top of the cookie base and refrigerate until set. You should allow 5 hours, to be on the safe side, and in fact this cake tastes better after a couple of days. The fragrance of the honey and orange really come through.

4 To make the oranges in syrup, heat the orange and lime juices with the water, honey, and cardamom, stirring from time to time to help the honey melt. Bring to a boil and cook for about 5 minutes, or until the mixture is quite syrupy. Leave to cool. Cut the top and bottom off each of the oranges then set them on a board and remove the peel and pith by slicing it off with a very sharp knife. Cut in a curve, working from top to bottom, all round each orange. Slice the oranges, flicking out any pips as you go, then put them into a shallow serving bowl and pour the cooled honey syrup over the top.

5 Unmould the cheesecake and scatter with the chopped pistachios. Sift a little confectioner's sugar on top and serve with the oranges.

"Bread makes itself, by your kindness, with your help, with imagination running through you, with dough under your hand, you are breadmaking itself..."

EDWARD ESPE BROWN, *THE TASSAJARA BREAD BOOK*

FOOD FROM THE HEARTH

FLATBREADS

I'm not one of those purist cooks who believe that you have to do everything yourself – I have never crafted my own sausages, dried my own fruit or made vinegar from the dregs of my guests' leftover wine. Cooking should be about pleasure, not exhaustion, and there are some great food producers whose experience and skill you can never hope to better. But some foods *are* worth making yourself, either because you can't get a good commercial version or because the thrill of doing it, and the results, far outweigh the effort. So it is with flatbreads. If you don't have a decent Turkish bakery at the end of your road (and most of us don't), or you'd like to take something out of your oven which is so earthy and basic that it feels like the first food ever cooked, then read on.

Flatbreads are everywhere. Fluffy naans and duvet-like focaccia, crispy pizzas, pockets of pita and crêpe-like tortillas all come under the "flatbread" heading. They're really user-friendly foods: great dippers, scooper uppers, wrappers, and bases for other ingredients. But most of the flatbreads we eat are processed and, frankly, they're not much good. As far as supermarket pita is concerned, you'd be better off eating cardboard. Yet bread is the mainstay of the Middle Eastern meal, honored by being the focus of the beggar's cry, "Give me bread in the name of Allah". In many Arab countries it is picked up and cleaned if it falls on the floor. Loaves and sheets of bread are considered so special that people take considerable time buying them or are immensely proud of their skill if they make them. They believe every bit of bread is unique, as Elias Canetti writes in *The Voices of Marrakesh*:

"In the evenings, after dark, I went to that part of the Djemaa el-Fna where the women sold bread. They squatted on the ground in a long line... From time to time each would pick up a loaf of bread in her right hand, toss it a little way into the air, catch it again, tilt it to and fro a few times as if weighing it, give it a couple of audible pats, and then, these caresses completed, put it back on top of the other loaves. In this way the loaf itself, its freshness and weight and smell, as it were, offered themselves for sale."

I yearn for bread like this – earthy, chewy dough to dip in the juices of a *tajine*, scoop up *mezze* or wrap around a wedge of spiced grilled meat. I want the pita breads you get in Lebanese restaurants, hot from the oven, soft and cloud-light, puffed up like a genie's slippers. And I want sheets of Iranian *lavash* and *taftoon*, oatmeal-colored and flecked with charring looking like ancient bits of papyrus or huge pieces of plaster from some crumbling building, they demand to be torn, forcing you back to the world of their birth.

When I started to experiment and talk to cooks and bakers, I found that the flatbread world was even bigger than I had supposed. Despite their name, flatbreads are not always flat – they can, like focaccia, be quite deep and soft, or they can be as thin as a crêpe. Some flatbreads include yeast or bicarbonate of soda to help them rise; others have no raising agent at all. Funnily enough, some of the thinnest flatbreads are actually leavened, the effect experienced in the softly textured, pliable nature of the bread rather than in its height.

Some flatbreads are baked in the oven, some are fried and some are cooked on a griddle or a terracotta stone. These breads are among the oldest foods we eat. Presumably somebody arrived at the idea by leaving a porridge of pounded grain and water to dry out, or by accidentally baking a slab of the porridge on a hot stone, and flatbread was born. We know that the Egyptians, those "bread-eaters" of the ancient world, made flatbreads. The ingredients and methods are still very much the same now as they were then. Like all breads, flatbreads are simple. They are made of flour, water, salt, and perhaps leavening. But flatbreads are much quicker to cook than big loaves, so they use less fuel. And their shape lends itself to being used as both plate and eating utensil, so you don't need anything else to complete your meal. For these reasons, flatbreads have always been the cheapest and most practical choice for peasants and nomadic people.

Italian focaccia was around well before ovens appeared on the scene. The dough was simply slapped on to a stone slab, flattened, and covered with embers. Some Moroccan breads, even today, are cooked in a hole under the hot desert sands, and Iranians still make "pebble bread": a lovely bubbly-textured bread that is cooked on, and indented by, small, hot, round stones. Other flatbreads are baked in ovens whose shape and design hasn't changed for centuries, such as the *tonir*, used to make *taftoon*. *Tonirs* are exactly the same as Indian *tandoor* ovens: barrel-shaped, open at the top and heated at the base by coal, wood or gas (or camel dung if it's handy). In Iran, bakers use a special pillow to slap the round of dough onto the hot oven walls, where it cooks in minutes.

If you're not pressed for time, it's a pleasure to cook any bread. The dough feels lovely in your hands, like the most yielding pillow and, when kneaded, as soft and smooth as a baby's cheek. But making flatbreads gives added pleasure because they are such old foods. It's like cooking pieces of history. Perhaps this is why we balk at making them ourselves. We suspect they can only be cooked in the alleys of Cairo, Fez or Istanbul, kneaded by dark, robed men whose understanding of the mystique of bread has been absorbed from birth. It's true that these practitioners are brilliant at their craft, but it's a long way to go for a piece of pita, and you can easily learn to turn out a passable imitation. Flatbreads are one of the oldest foods we cook and the most ancient foods employ the simplest cooking methods.

The main disadvantage of cooking these breads at home is that domestic ovens never get as hot as professional or wood-fired ones. But if you put your baking sheet or pizza stone into a hot oven a good thirty minutes before you intend to cook the flatbreads, you can make a pretty good job of replicating those searing-hot surfaces. Some flatbreads also adapt well to being cooked on a hot griddle, so you can try different methods and see which you prefer.

There are a few things that I've tripped up on in my bread-making history. Although flatbreads don't rise as much as regular loaves, the same rules apply. Make sure that your yeast is active by leaving it to froth before adding it to the other ingredients. Too much salt, fat or sugar will inhibit the yeast's ability to work or kill it altogether, so don't add any more of these than indicated in the recipe. It's difficult to be precise about the amount of water you need in any bread, as this depends on the age of the flour and even on how humid the weather is, so add enough water just to bring your dough together and add any more a tablespoonful at a time. You don't want to end up adding extra flour to save a soggy dough, as this will upset the balance of yeast to flour. If you're kneading by hand there's no shortcut – you've got to develop the gluten in the flour so that it can stretch and hold, trapping the air you're incorporating and the carbon dioxide that makes the bread rise. You'll need to work at your dough for about 15 minutes, until it is smooth and elastic and bounces back when you prod it with your finger. If you use a mixer with a dough-hook to knead your bread, don't overwork it – about seven minutes is fine – or the strands of gluten can become overextended and break.

When I'm too lazy to use even the dough-hook, I make really quick unyeasted flatbreads, sometimes as substitutes for their more time-consuming relations. *Piadina* is an Italian flatbread from Emilia-Romagna that you often see wrapped around salami or prosciutto on bar counters. There's no rising time with *piadina*, so you can make it in a jiffy. You still get the salty, charred taste of pizza, though with a different texture, and I use *piadina* in much the same way, even though it's more often used as a wrap in its homeland. I also serve *piadina* instead of Arab bread, especially if I'm short of time. It feels good to have something warm and doughy on the table in less time than it takes to cook a pan of pasta. *Socca*, made from a chickpea-flour batter, could barely be called a bread at all, since it requires no rising or kneading and isn't doughy; it's really more like a thick crêpe. Although *socca's* cooked in huge shallow pans in its native Nice, it works well as smaller individual cakes, making a really nutty-tasting base for strong-flavored foods. And it takes about 10 minutes to make!

The great thing about all these flatbreads is just how much you can do with them. Top a round of *piadina* with sausage and roasted peppers, or grilled radicchio and smoked mozzarella, or a simple salad of tomato and basil moistened with enough olive oil to soak into the dough. Make your own kind of eastern garlic bread by brushing rounds of Arab flatbread with *zahtar* – a paste of thyme, sesame seeds, sumac, and garlic mixed with olive oil – before you bake it, pricking it with a fork to ensure it doesn't balloon. Try *socca* with other Provençal flavors: *anchoïade* or *tapenade*, goat cheese, red mullet, or sautéed squid with garlic. You'll also find that *socca* goes well with anything flavored with cumin or coriander, maybe not surprisingly since chickpea flour is used in Indian cooking. And those wonderful Middle Eastern pocket breads, such as pita, serve as pouches for so many things. Stuff them with hummus, grilled peppers or eggplants, spiced chicken or lamb, feta cheese, olives, cucumbers, and fresh cilantro, yogurt and pickled chilies… where do I end? There is no end. Flatbreads have been around for millennia, and they'll be here for a long time to come. They're the most basic, usable, easy-to-make example of the staff of life. Don't leave them to supermarkets and fast-food joints; get your oven on.

SOCCA WITH SARDINES, ROAST TOMATOES, AND OLIVE AND PARSLEY SALAD

*An old Niçois specialty made of nothing more than chickpea flour, water, and oil,
socca is like a big thick pancake. In Nice, socca's cooked in broad, shallow pans
and sold in hot, peppered wedges at little stalls and mobile carts. It's rumored to
be the favorite pick-me-up of builders working in the city. Nobody ever makes
socca at home in Nice — it's very much a street food. The Niçois usually like it
unadulterated, but some local chefs — looking for a spin on traditional cooking —
strew it with other Provençal flavors: tomatoes, peppers, olives, anchovies, and even
goat cheese. The nutty earthiness of socca goes well with these vibrant tastes, so it
makes a great base. It's also very easy to cook.*

serves 4

12 roast tomatoes (*see* p132)

olive oil for frying

8 good-sized sardines, scaled
    and gutted

salt and pepper

lemon wedges for serving

FOR THE OLIVE AND

PARSLEY SALAD

5½ oz black olives (preferably
    Niçois), pitted

½ red onion, very finely chopped

1 medium bunch flat-leaf
    parsley, roughly chopped

1 garlic clove, finely chopped

juice of ¼ lemon

4 tbsp extra-virgin olive oil

FOR THE *SOCCA* BATTER

6oz chickpea flour

1¾ cups (14fl oz) water

5 tbsp olive oil

1 To make the olive and parsley salad, mix everything together, season with
salt and pepper, and leave at room temperature so the flavors meld together.

2 For the roast tomatoes, follow the instructions on p132.

3 To make the *socca*, put the chickpea flour in a large bowl and gradually add
the water and olive oil, whisking to make a smooth batter. Season with salt
and pepper and set aside for half an hour.

4 To cook the *socca*, heat 1½ tsp of olive oil in a frying pan. Using a quarter
of the chickpea mixture for each pancake, pour the batter into the frying pan
once the oil is really hot. Turn the heat down a bit and let the *socca* cook,
turning it over once it is well-colored on the bottom and firm. These are not
like French crêpes — they are not supposed to be light and thin, but quite
thick and substantial. Add a little more oil to the pan for each pancake and
keep the cooked ones warm.

5 Give the sardines a good wash, making sure you get rid of any traces of
blood. Dry them and season them inside and out. Cook them — either in a
little olive oil in a frying pan or, brushed with a little oil, on a ridged griddle
pan about 6 minutes on each side, or until cooked through. If you can do
them on the barbecue, even better.

6 Serve each person with a *socca* pancake topped with the salad, a few roast
tomatoes, a couple of sardines, and lemon wedges.

LAMB PIZZA WITH PRESERVED LEMONS

Known as Lahma bi Ajeen *in the Lebanon and* Lahmacun *in Turkey, you find versions of this all over the Middle East. Some are tomato-based, some add pomegranate molasses or tamarind, and some have pine nuts. You can alter the dish every time you make it. I like it with slivers of preserved lemon and little nuggets of yogurt — it's a wonderful blend of spiced-lamb sweetness and clean-cut sourness.*

serves 6 as a main course with salad

1 quantity of Noura's Khobz
  flatbread (*see* p156), made
  without the milk powder

olive oil

FOR THE LAMB

2lb lean lamb, minced

4 garlic cloves, crushed

2 tsp ground cumin

2 tsp ground cinnamon

½ tsp ground caraway

4 tsp *harissa* (*see* p19)

salt

FOR THE ONION

2 onions, finely sliced

2 tbsp olive oil

9 plum tomatoes, chopped

2 tsp ground cinnamon

1 tsp ground allspice

TO SERVE

½ preserved lemon (*see* p165)

a bunch of cilantro,
  roughly chopped

Greek yogurt (optional)

1 Mix all the ingredients for the lamb together, cover and put in the fridge.

2 Make the dough according to the instructions on p156. Once the dough has risen and you have punched it back, divide it into six balls. Using extra flour, roll these into six long, oval shapes. Put these on well-floured baking sheets, cover these loosely with plastic wrap or a dish towel, and set them aside to prove for 20 minutes.

3 Put baking sheets, pizza stones or unglazed quarry tiles into an oven, preheated to 475°F, or as hot as you can get it.

4 Sauté the sliced onions in the olive oil. Once they are softening, add the tomatoes and cook for another 5 minutes. Stir in the cinnamon and allspice and cook everything for a couple of minutes more. The mixture shouldn't be wet.

5 Pit the surface of each pizza lightly with your fingers and divide the onion and tomato mixture among them. Spread it over the top, leaving about an inch around the outside.

6 Put little nuggets of lamb all over the pizzas and drizzle with a little olive oil. If you're using metal baking sheets, lightly oil them by rubbing them with oil-moistened paper towels or brushing them with a pastry brush. Slide the pizzas onto the hot baking sheets or stones. Cook for about 8 minutes (less if your oven goes to a higher temperature) until the bread is cooked but soft.

7 Remove the flesh from the preserved lemon and slice the rind into fine strips. Scatter the rind over the pizzas along with the cilantro. Daub with a little Greek yogurt if you like, and serve.

TURKISH PIZZA WITH POMEGRANATES, SPINACH, AND FETA

Yes, there is pizza in Turkey, and these are particularly beautiful. With the green of the spinach and the pink of the pomegranates, they look like fading roses.

*serves 4 as a main course
with salad*

FOR THE BASE

2 tsp dried yeast

½ tsp superfine sugar

⅝ cup (5fl oz) lukewarm water

12oz strong all-purpose flour

½ tsp salt

1fl oz milk

1½fl oz olive oil

FOR THE TOPPING

1lb 2oz spinach

olive oil

1 red onion, finely chopped

3 garlic cloves, crushed

salt and pepper

6oz feta cheese, crumbled

1oz pine nuts

seeds from 1 pomegranate

1 For the base, mix the yeast with the sugar and a little of the warm water. Stir and leave somewhere warm for about 15 minutes, until the liquid froths.

2 Sift the flour and salt into a bowl and make a well in the center. Pour the yeast into this, mixing in the flour from around the sides as you do so. Gradually add the milk and the olive oil and finish with as much of the remaining water as it takes to bind everything.

3 Knead the dough until smooth – about 10 minutes. Rub a little extra olive oil over the surface of the dough, put it in a clean bowl, cover with a damp cloth and leave in a warm place for 1½ hours.

4 For the topping, de-stalk and wash the spinach leaves and cook them, in the water that still clings to them, on a low heat in a covered saucepan. It will take about 4 minutes. Turn the leaves over a couple of times so that the spinach at the bottom of the pan doesn't catch. When the spinach is cooked, squeeze out the moisture and chop roughly.

5 Heat 2 tbsp of olive oil in a frying pan and cook the onion over a gentle heat until it is just softening. Add the garlic, spinach, and seasoning and cook for another 4-5 minutes, stirring from time to time. You need to get the spinach quite dry so that you don't end up with a soggy pizza.

6 Put either pizza stones or metal baking sheets into the oven to heat at 425°F.

7 Knock back the pizza dough and separate it into four balls. Using a little extra flour, roll each of these into an irregular pizza shape – the Turks like misshapen ovals. Put these on lightly floured baking sheets. Cover loosely with clingfilm and leave to prove for another half an hour.

8 Divide the spinach mixture between the pizzas and top with the feta. Drizzle with a little olive oil. Lightly oil the baking sheets if you're using them, and transfer the pizzas on to the sheets or hot stones and cook for 5 minutes. Scatter the pine nuts on top and cook for another 3 minutes until the dough is firm and lightly colored. Don't overcook these or the dough will become horribly hard. Scatter the pomegranate seeds and black pepper over the top and serve.

MEZZE WITH NOURA'S KHOBZ

Noura, a Lebanese restaurant in London, is one of my favorite places to eat, and their bread, known as khobz, *comes to the table in great warm pillows. Ziad Sawaya who, on a busy day, can churn out a thousand of these breads, gave me his recipe plus a bit of tuition. You can serve this with any* mezze, *but this is a good sweet-salty mix.*

serves 4 -6

FOR THE BREAD

2 tsp dried yeast

1 tsp superfine sugar

1¾ cups (14fl oz)
    lukewarm water

1lb 10oz white bread flour

2¼oz milk powder

1½ tsp salt

1 tbsp olive oil

FOR THE *HOURIYA*

10½oz carrots

1½ tsp ground cumin

2 tsp *harissa* (*see* p19)

½ tbsp white-wine vinegar

juice of 1 lime

1½ tsp honey

5 tbsp extra-virgin olive oil

salt and pepper

FOR THE MASHED FETA

2¾ oz feta cheese

1¼ cups (10fl oz) Greek yogurt

3 tbsp olive oil

1 garlic clove, crushed

2 tbsp dill, chopped

2 tbsp mint, chopped

FOR THE SALAD

1 portion of the olive and
    parsley salad (*see* p150)

½ preserved lemon (*see* p165)

1 To make the bread, mix the yeast with the sugar and 3½fl oz of the water. Leave it in a warm place to froth for about 15 minutes.

2 Sift the dry ingredients for the bread into a bowl and make a well in the center. Pour the yeast into the middle and start bringing in all the dry ingredients from around the outside. Add the oil and as much of the rest of the water as you need to bring everything together. The dough should be quite soft and tacky. Knead for 10-15 minutes until it is shiny. Cover loosely and put it in a warm place to rise for 1½ hours.

3 To make the *houriya*, cut the carrots into chunks and cook until they're tender. Drain and purée in a food processor with all the other ingredients. Taste – you may want to add more salt or pepper, honey or vinegar. Let the mixture cool.

4 For the mashed feta, simply mash all of the ingredients together. It should be quite lumpy.

5 For the salad, cut the rind of the preserved lemon into slivers and mix it with the olive salad. Leave so that the flavors can meld.

6 When the dough has doubled in size, punch it back. Divide it into eight balls and, using extra flour, roll them out to about ¹⁄₁₆ inch in thickness. Put these on floured baking sheets, cover loosely with plastic wrap, and leave to prove for about half an hour.

7 Put the baking sheets, unglazed quarry tiles or pizza stones, into an oven preheated to 475°F, or as hot as you can get it.

8 When you're ready to serve, lightly oil the metal sheets if you're using them, then slide the bread on to these, or the pizza stones, and sprinkle with water. Bake in the oven for about 7 minutes. The bread should balloon and remain soft and pliable.

9 Give each of the *mezze* a final drizzle of extra-virgin olive oil and serve with the bread.

PIADINA WITH CARAMELIZED ONIONS, WALNUTS, AND TALEGGIO

Piadina is an Italian flatbread (from Emilia-Romagna) that isn't made with yeast, so it is ultra-quick to turn out. It's thinner and crisper than pizza but has the same scorched bread flavor. You mostly find it used as a wrap in Italy, but it works really well as an alternative pizza base. It's one of those speedy breads that will have the kitchen smelling of cooked dough in less time than it would take to boil a saucepan of pasta.

serves 4

FOR THE BREAD

1lb 2oz bread flour, sifted

½ tsp salt

2 tbsp olive oil

water

FOR THE ONIONS

2 tbsp olive oil

½ oz unsalted butter

5 medium onions, very
   finely sliced

leaves from a sprig of
   rosemary, chopped

salt and pepper

1 tbsp balsamic vinegar

TO FINISH

9oz taleggio cheese,
   thinly sliced

3½oz shelled walnuts,
   roughly chopped

1 For the bread, mix the flour with the salt and then gradually start adding the olive oil and enough water to make a dough. Knead for 10 minutes until it is smooth. Cover the dough while you get on with everything else.

2 Heat the oil and butter together in a heavy-bottomed saucepan and add the onions. Stir them around to make sure they all get coated in the fat and continue to cook them over a medium heat until they are starting to become translucent, stirring from time to time. Turn the heat down low, add about 2 tbsp water to the onions (this will stop them catching during their long, slow cooking), sprinkle on the rosemary, and cover the pot. Cook the onions for 45-60 minutes – the time it takes seems to depend on the sweetness of the onions – stirring from time to time, until they are beginning to caramelize. Add another splash of water if it looks as though the onions might burn.

3 When the onions are completely soft, season them, turn up the heat, and stir. Add the balsamic vinegar as you do this. When they're a deep, dark brown, take the onions off the heat, cover, and leave them while you cook the *piadina*.

4 Divide the dough into four and roll each ball into a round – it can be quite misshapen. Heat a griddle until it is very hot, then cook each round on both sides. It is fine to have patches of lightly charred dough. Prick the dough if it starts to rise and bubble.

5 Spread onions on each *piadina*, top with the slices of cheese and scatter with the walnuts. Put under a hot broiler until the cheese starts to bubble, and serve with a rocket or watercress salad.

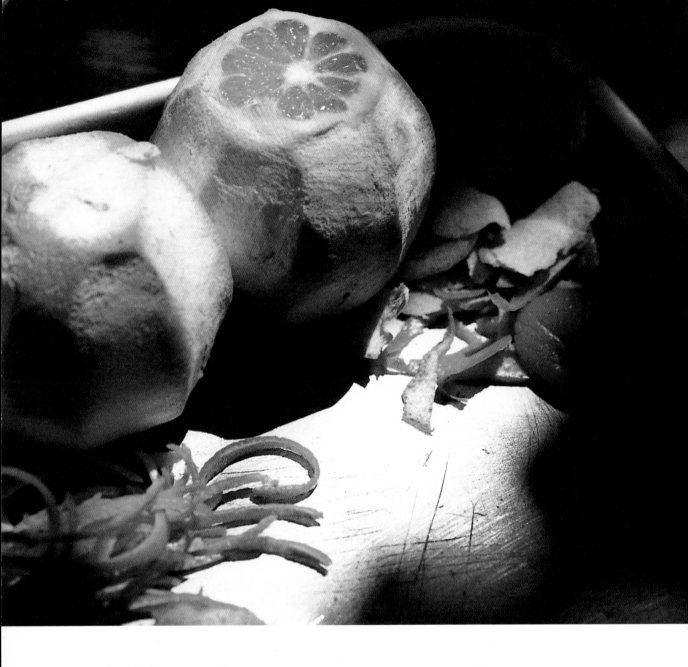

"When there comes a cluster of orange trees,

the oranges are red like coals among the

darker leaves. But lemons, lemons,

innumerable, speckled like innumerable tiny

stars in the green firmament of leaves..."

D. H. LAWRENCE, *SEA AND SARDINIA*

PITH AND SKIN

ORANGES AND LEMONS

When I was little I used to consume a lot of an orange drink called "Tree Top". The label featured a photograph of an orange tree: a network of dark, Christmas-green leaves, vivid little fiery globes, and white blossom. I loved the picture; I used to sit on the floor and stare at it. But its beauty didn't seem to have anything to do with the oranges I ate – or rather, didn't eat. In our house we all fought over the portioning of strawberries, peaches, and nectarines and even took an interest in the different varieties of apples that came and went, but bananas and oranges? Nah. There were always plenty of them; no need to get excited.

Then, on a school visit to Mallorca, we took a trip on a rickety train – all rattling wooden carriages and no windowpanes – from Palma to Soller. The route cut through the centre of the island and, quite unexpectedly, my breath was taken away by the view through the window. We were in the middle of orange groves, acres of them; I could even put my hand out the window and touch them. They were so beautiful that they didn't seem real. "Surely these are trees for dolls," I thought. Both leaves and oranges looked like they had been carved from wood, stained and polished. Suddenly the orange assumed all the exoticism of the mango. Soon after this, I began to fancy myself as the girl in the Leonard Cohen song who sipped her tea with oranges "that came all the way from China" (which is where they did originally come from) and began to taste and appreciate those fluorescent mounds that sat on the grocery shelves. I have loved oranges ever since, especially as they are at their best just when you need them: in the middle of winter. Whoever was responsible for designing nature, this was one of their more inspired touches.

It was the bitter, or Seville, orange (the one still used for making marmalade) that arrived in the Mediterranean first. Like so many foods, it was brought there by the Arabs. In fact, the path of the conquering forces of Islam, as they swept their way across to North Africa and up into Spain and Sicily, is marked in citrus groves. The Arabs planted glowing terraces of orange trees in Sicily; squares of them against the whitewashed walls of Sevillian courtyards; avenues of them in the great Muslim palaces. Orange trees had the power to enchant. French kings started building orangeries and importing the trees from Italy, bathing the roots in milk and honey before planting them in pots with wheels. These would be wheeled outside so that the trees, like exotic royalty, could enjoy the warmth of sunny days, returning to their glasshouse when the coolness of late afternoon descended. The Medici incorporated oranges into their coat of arms, and Renaissance painters, quite inaccurately, started sticking orange trees behind Christ and the Virgin Mary. For a long time it was oranges-a-go-go, the fruits admired as much for their beauty and fragrance as for their taste.

The orange's popularity as a food really took off when the sweet version arrived on the scene, grown first by the Portuguese. But it's in the countries where the Arabs planted the bitter orange that you still find the most interesting orange dishes. Sicilians mix the rind and juice with nuts and raisins to stuff sardines, and serve grilled tuna with a sweet-sour orange sauce; Andalusians cook duck with green olives and oranges and will offer you a wedge to squeeze over a veal chop; Moroccans sprinkle sliced oranges with flower water and cinnamon for the easiest dessert in the world; and both the Italians and the Spanish make wonderful salads with oranges, putting the sweetest specimens against inky black olives, cleansing fennel, woody sherry vinegar, and even raw salt cod. For a truly grown-up appreciation of the orange just slice some good navel oranges, layer them with wafer-thin red onions, and anoint the whole thing with extra-virgin olive oil. It might sound like summer eating, but these salads bring great shocks of sunshine to wintering taste buds.

It isn't always easy to find good oranges, as appearance is no indication of flavor. A perfectly formed glowing little orb can taste pallid. A pale, misshapen, pockmarked one can be delicious. Valencia oranges have a smooth, thick skin (which makes them good for zesting) and are juicy, but navels – they're the ones with a belly button in one end – are the best for flavor. They're definitely "the only fruit" – mouth-puckeringly citrus-y, easy to peel, and almost seedless. And the Sicilian raspberry-hued, blood orange – that once-a-year treat? Don't get me started: scarlet, sweet, stunning. May they always be an occasional joy.

The most sensible thing to do is buy a couple of oranges at a time from the supermarket and, if they're good, go back the next day and buy a big bag of the same batch. The navels I got this winter were so good that some nights I didn't even cook; I just set a bag of navel oranges on the sofa and ate them in front of the TV.

I'm not one for fancy orange desserts. Let this fruit be itself. I simply want slices or segments bathed in light citrus-fruit syrups flavored with lime and cardamom, orange-flower water, mint, rosemary, even tarragon. They're also good in the kind of spicy red-wine syrup in which you usually poach pears. And don't let anyone tell you that oranges in caramel is an abomination of the '70s. Done well (I mean with tasty oranges and a syrup that isn't burnt) it's a great dish; made with blood oranges, it's spectacular. These oranges-in-syrup dishes are good with oranges alone, but some of them are even better with the additional colors and flavors that grapefruit, blood orange, and pomelo bring. It's lovely to see the various shades floating in a bowl together.

Sorbets and *granitas* are two of the best ways to get a mouthful of pure citrus essence. Grapefruit with mint produces a sorbet that looks, and refreshes, like a glassful of snow; blood orange mixed with pomegranate juice and vodka makes a stunning *granita* of garnet shards and glassy seeds; orange and mandarin are great by themselves.

Cakes give you the chance to take advantage of the orange's perfume rather than its zing. The perfume is in the rind – you can see sprays of the oil when you peel an orange – and that's what a cake needs. You can kid yourself by adding more juice in place of rind, but you won't get away with it. And if you're going to use peel, buy unwaxed organic oranges. I know they say you can scrub wax off, but starting a recipe with a brush and washing up liquid is not my idea of a good time – and that goes for lemons, too.

Ah, lemons… They could never be a "second-best", neither in the culinary nor the visual stakes. One early Arab poet described the oranges of Sicily as "blazing emerald fires among the emerald boughs" while the lemons, in comparison, wore "the paleness of a lover who has spent the night crying…" It's doubtful whether even lack of love could diminish the lemon, though. I'm fond of the odd roller-coaster ride for my taste buds such as, Mexican-style, sucking a bit of salted lemon or lime and then throwing a shot of Tequila down my throat. My three-year-old likes the same kind of shock, as he puckers and grimaces in delight, chewing on a lemon slice stolen from a jug of lemonade. Sicilians, mind you, will slice a piece of fresh lemon, salt it, and chew it without so much as a quiver. It's good to remind yourself of the power of lemon: so much more than just a fruit, but a seasoning as potent as salt or sugar, a flavor-heightener *par excellence*. When something seems to be missing from a dish, the hidden element can often be found by the lemon. It works in mysterious ways, making the parsley in a parsley sauce taste greener, mangoes taste sweeter, and rose water more floral and less cloying. Lemon makes nearly everything taste more of itself. Fish is nothing without lemon – it brings out the sweetness and restores the taste of the sea – but try it squeezed on steak and grilled lamb, too.

Lemon's sharp juice sours and tenderizes, too. Few dishes in the Middle Eastern kitchen escape this fruit – marinating cubes of lamb, high-octane salads of parsley and onion, purées of chickpeas and eggplants all bear its stamp, and North African cooks even treat lemons whole, subduing their astringency by draining out some of their acidity with salt. Once preserved, the brightness of lemons turns a mellow, translucent gold. Their flavor is salty and slightly sour, but they have none of the rasping acidity of fresh lemons. Make a jar and you'll soon be addicted to the taste, employing them not just in Moroccan *tajines*, but in a dish of Mediterranean vegetables, with olive oil-roasted potatoes and red onions, in bowls of bulgar wheat, couscous, and pulses. Or try preserved peel, in place of grated rind, with finely chopped parsley and garlic for a twist on the Italian *gremolata* for a deeper, richer addition to meaty, tomatoey stews. In Egypt a bowl of preserved lemons is often served with *mezze*, so each diner can take quarters to eat with pulses, particularly the bean dish *ful medames*.

Pickling lemon slices is another way to preserve and soften the fruit's character. Salt cut lemons overnight, then layer them in a jar with stripes of paprika and bathe them in olive oil. They will glow on the shelves of your pantry, suggesting possibilities the other jars never could. I often use them as I would preserved lemons, remembering that the paprika gives them an additional kick: chop them up with black olives and parsley for a salad or add them to a braise of chicken or lamb. Lay whole slices on fish filets and bake in the oven, or tuck them into a pan full of chicken joints and wedges of red onion for roasting. And don't forget the lemon-infused oil; it's brilliant for vinaigrettes.

Oranges provide a culinary wake-up call; lemons are indispensable. And even if you're not in the mood for cooking, it's still worth giving in to the impulse to buy those big bags of citrus color. Just pile the oranges in one bowl, the lemons in another, and put them somewhere prominent. The beauty of some foods is as important as the taste.

LAMB AND ORANGE KHORESH

Khoresht are Persian stews, although the Persians themselves think of them as "sauces" to dress big bowls of plain white rice. Made with meat, fish or vegetables, and usually containing large amounts of herbs or fruits, they're often sour, or at least sour-sweet, using lemon juice, powdered limes, tamarind or pomegranates to achieve this characteristic taste. There are some wonderful pairings — lamb with rhubarb and mint; fish with walnuts and pomegranates; chicken with apricots and saffron. They are quite like sour-sweet Moroccan tajines and it's thought that the Arabs, who conquered Persia, carried the idea to North Africa. I always feel a bit like a sorceress when I'm cooking these stews — they're so unusual and exotic.

serves 6

3 oranges

1½oz unsalted butter

2 tsp superfine sugar

olive oil

1½lb lamb from the leg, cut
    into (1-1½in) cubes

2 onions, finely chopped

1 tsp ground cinnamon

seeds from 3 cardamom
    pods, ground

1¼ cups (10fl oz) orange juice

juice of 1 lime

1¼ cups (10fl oz) lamb stock
    or water

salt and pepper

3 carrots

a good handful of mint
    leaves, torn

2 tsp orange-flower water

1oz shelled pistachios,
    roughly chopped or slivered

1 Remove the peel from the oranges, taking care to leave the pith behind, and cut it into fine strips about the size of a match. Cover with cold water, bring to the boil, cook for 2 minutes, then strain. Heat half the butter in a small pan and add the orange rind. Stir, then add the sugar and cook over a medium heat for a couple of minutes, until the sugar has melted and the rind has lightly caramelized. Set aside.

2 Heat 2 tbsp of the olive oil in a heavy-bottomed casserole. Fry the lamb cubes over a fairly high heat, so that they get a good browning on the outside. You should do this in batches to ensure that they get properly colored. Set the lamb aside.

3 Add another 1 tbsp olive oil to the pan with the rest of the butter. Heat this and sauté the onion until soft and translucent. Sprinkle on the cinnamon and cardamom and cook for another minute. Add the juices, stock or water, and the lamb, together with any juices that have run out of it. Season and bring to the boil. Turn down to a simmer, cover the pan, and cook the lamb on a very low heat for 1¼ hours.

4 Peel the carrots and cut them into fine strips, about 2½ inches long. Using a very sharp knife, remove the white pith from each of the oranges then, cutting close to the membrane, remove each segment. Add the carrots to the lamb for the last 20 minutes of cooking time, and the orange segments for the last 10 minutes. Gently stir in the orange rind and half the mint during the last couple of minutes.

5 Stir the orange-flower water into the *khoresh* and either turn it into a heated bowl or serve it in the pot in which it has been cooked, scattered with the rest of the mint and the pistachios. It doesn't need a fussy accompaniment — just serve it with plain white rice, as in Iran.

"The dominant theme in English cuisine is the use of spices for their own sake, especially in pursuit of effects that — and this is the real key to the historic national palate — combine the sour and the sweet."

JOHN LANCHESTER, *THE DEBT TO PLEASURE*

PORK WITH FETA AND SPINACH STUFFING AND CARDAMOM-SPICED ORANGES

This is a Greek-inspired dish, and a great alternative to more prosaic stuffed roast pork. You can serve almost any starch on the side — couscous, bulgar wheat, brown rice or potatoes. The recipe makes more spiced oranges than you need for this dish, but keep the rest in the refrigerator and eat them with duck, cold ham, pork or pâté.

serves 6-8

1 x 4lb (boned weight)
   loin of pork
½ large onion, finely chopped
olive oil
1lb 2oz spinach
6oz feta cheese, cubed
salt and pepper
coarsely ground sea salt

FOR THE ORANGES
5 thin-skinned oranges
1⅞ cups (15fl oz) water
½ cup (4fl oz)
   white-wine vinegar
12oz superfine sugar
1 tsp fennel seeds
8 cardamom pods, bruised
6 cloves
½ cinnamon stick

1 Score the fat on the pork loin, cutting through the skin but not right through the fat, in a criss-cross pattern, and then spread the loin out ready for stuffing.

2 Sauté the onion in 2 tbsp of the olive oil until pale golden in color. Wash the spinach, remove the stalks, and cook the leaves in the water that's left clinging to them. This should take about 4 minutes over a medium heat in a covered saucepan. Squeeze the excess moisture from the spinach and chop it fairly finely.

3 Mix the onion, spinach, and feta together and season. Season the pork and spread the stuffing over it. Roll up the joint and secure with fine string. Drizzle the skin with a little olive oil and press the coarse sea salt on it. Cook in an oven preheated to 425°F for half an hour, then reduce the heat to 375°F and cook for a further 1 hour 40 minutes.

4 Meanwhile, halve the oranges horizontally and cut each half into about eight half-moon-shaped slices, flicking out any pips.

5 Put all the other ingredients for the oranges in a saucepan and heat gently, stirring from time to time until the sugar has melted. Bring to the boil and simmer for 5 minutes, then add the oranges. Simmer them for about 40 minutes, until the skins are tender. Leave the oranges to cool in the syrup.

6 When the pork is cooked, move it to a heated serving dish, cover, and keep warm for 10 minutes while it rests. Serve the pork with any juices poured over it and the oranges alongside it.

PICKLED LEMONS

Very few pickles are as simple to make as this, or pack such a punch. Use them in any of the dishes in which you would use preserved lemons (remembering that you've got the added flavor of paprika here), or serve slices with grilled fish, chicken or fatty lamb chops. Use thin-skinned lemons if you can.

organic, unwaxed lemons

coarse sea salt

paprika

extra-virgin olive oil

1 Wash and slice the lemons. Put the slices in a colander set over a bowl, sprinkling with salt as you go. Leave overnight to drain off the moisture.

2 Layer the lemon slices in a jar, sprinkling paprika between each layer, until the jar is full. Cover with extra-virgin olive oil. They'll be ready to eat in about three weeks.

PRESERVED LEMONS

These great golden ovals of flavor are a bit of an acquired taste, but once you get used to them it's easy to become addicted. Slivers of rind are great with Mediterranean vegetables, or stirred through pulses, couscous or rice; chopped quarters can be added to meaty roasts, and a dash of the preserving juices will lift a casserole or vinaigrette. Use thin-skinned lemons if possible.

organic, unwaxed lemons

coarse sea salt

a couple of cinnamon sticks

2 tsp cilantro seeds

½ tsp black peppercorns

2 or 3 bay leaves

fresh lemon juice

olive oil

1 Wash the lemons well and quarter each one lengthwise, but don't cut all the way through. You should end up with lemons that open like flowers. Take each one and, holding it half open, put 2 tsp of salt into it. Squeeze it closed and put into a sterilized jar. Do this with all the lemons you want to preserve, then put a weight – like a clean stone – on top of them, cover with a lid, and leave them in a warm place for a few days while the juices run out.

2 Remove the weight and add the cinnamon sticks, cilantro seeds, peppercorns, and bay leaves. Add enough fresh lemon juice to cover the lemons completely – this is very important – then pour a layer of olive oil on top. The lemons will be ready to use in about a month.

SPICED CHICKEN ON MELTING ONIONS WITH PRESERVED LEMON

I love all the dishes in this book but, if I haven't had it for a while, my version of this Moroccan tajine is the one I crave. The odd perfume of saffron mixed with the sweet meatiness of green olives and the sour saltiness of preserved lemons just isn't like any European dish. In an authentic tajine, a whole chicken would be cooked, without browning, in stock and spices until the flesh falls off the bone. This version is quicker and preserves the fresh flavors of the ingredients. If you can, get cracked olives, where the flesh has been slit, allowing the flavors to penetrate.

serves 4

4 chicken breast joints, skin
    on and partly boned
2 tbsp olive oil
3 onions, halved and sliced
    into half-moons
½ tsp ground turmeric
1 cup (8fl oz) chicken stock
    or water
½ tsp saffron threads
3oz green olives

FOR THE MARINADE
½ preserved lemon
6 garlic cloves, crushed
1 tsp ground ginger
½ tsp each of ground cumin,
    paprika, and cayenne pepper
4 tbsp olive oil
2 tbsp lemon oil (from the
    preserved lemons)
salt and pepper

To serve
a good handful of flat-leaf
    parsley or cilantro,
    roughly chopped

1 For the marinade, remove the flesh from the inside of the lemon and chop it up, retaining the outer rind to use in the sauce. Mix the flesh with all the other marinade ingredients.

2 Rub the marinade all over the chicken joints, spooning some marinade just under the skin if you can. Cover and leave in the refrigerator for at least 3 hours, or overnight. Turn the joints every so often.

3 Heat the olive oil in the bottom of a shallow, ovenproof pan. Add the chicken and quickly cook the outside until nice and golden. Put the chicken aside.

4 In the same pan, start to cook the onions. When they are softening and beginning to turn translucent, add the turmeric and continue to cook, stirring, for another minute. Bring the stock or water up to the boil and dissolve the saffron in it. Add this to the pan, along with the chicken pieces and any juices that have come out of them. It will look as if you don't have much liquid, but this is all it needs – the chicken will continue to get nice and golden on top while the sauce makes itself underneath.

5 Cook in an oven, preheated to 350°F, for 30 minutes. Cut the lemon rind into fine strips and add it to the dish with the olives 15 minutes before the end of the cooking time. (You'll need to rinse the olives if they're in brine, but if they're in olive oil just drain them.) Scatter with parsley or cilantro, and serve with rice, couscous or flatbread.

A TALE OF THREE ORANGES

Three salads that show just how grown-up oranges can be. Serve the savory ones as an appetizer or with something simple such as roast or grilled chicken. The sweet one is a Moroccan staple that I have fancified. There, you will often be served sliced oranges sprinkled with cinnamon and orange-flower water — simple and stunning — but I love the addition of honey and the texture of a syrupy glaze.

SICILIAN ORANGE SALAD

serves 4

juice of 1 small lemon

5 tbsp extra-virgin olive oil

salt and pepper

3 fennel bulbs

1 small red onion, finely sliced

5 juicy oranges

4½ oz black olives

1 Mix the lemon juice, olive oil, and seasoning together. Trim the fennel, reserving the feathery bits, and remove any tough outer leaves. Quarter the bulbs lengthwise and cut out the heart. Slice the fennel finely and throw it into the dressing. Finely chop the feathery bits and add them with the onion.

2 Slice the ends off the oranges so they are flat at the top and bottom. Set the orange on one of its bases and, with a small sharp knife, cut the peel and pith from the fruit in strips, working from top to bottom all the way round. Slice the oranges into rounds, reserving any juice that comes out and flicking out any seeds. Add the oranges and juice to the fennel and onions togther with the olives. Mix the salad gently and, if you have time, cover and chill for half an hour before serving. Serve with extra-virgin olive oil on the side.

ANDALUSIAN ORANGE SALAD

serves 4

1½ oz raisins

1 tbsp sherry vinegar

3 tbsp dry sherry

5 oranges

½ red onion, very finely sliced

a good handful of mint
  leaves, torn

extra-virgin olive oil

salt and pepper

3oz watercress or lamb's lettuce

1½ oz flaked almonds, toasted

FOR THE DRESSING

½ tsp clear honey

1 tbsp sherry vinegar

3 tbsp extra-virgin olive oil

1 Put the raisins into a small saucepan with the sherry vinegar and sherry. Heat to boiling, then take the pan off the heat immediately and leave the raisins to plump up for about 15 minutes.

2 Peel and slice the oranges as in the previous recipe and put them on a serving platter with the onion and mint, either in the center of the plate, or on one half of it. Mix the dressing ingredients together, season, and pour this over everything. Cover and leave the flavors to develop for about 20 minutes.

3 Drain the raisins, keeping the sherry and vinegar left behind. Add 1 tbsp of extra-virgin olive oil to the sherry and vinegar, plus a little seasoning, to make a dressing that just coats your salad leaves. Toss the leaves with this, then put them round, or beside, the oranges.

4 Scatter the raisins and toasted almonds over the oranges and drizzle with a little extra-virgin olive oil before serving.

SWEET MOROCCAN ORANGE SALAD

serves 4

½ cup (4fl oz) freshly
  squeezed orange juice

juice of ½ lemon

2½ tbsp orange-blossom honey

5 oranges

a small bunch of mint

20 moist dates

1 tbsp orange-flower water

confectioner's sugar
  for dusting

1 Put the juices and honey in a small saucepan and gently heat, stirring to help the honey melt. Bring to the boil and cook until the liquid has reduced by a third. Let this cool.

2 Remove the peel and slice the oranges as in the first recipe. Lay the slices, overlapping, on a plate or in the bottom of a very shallow bowl, adding some mint leaves as you go.

3 Stone the dates and chop them roughly – the chunks should be quite big. Scatter these on top of the oranges with a final sprinkling of mint leaves.

4 When the syrup is cold, add the orange-flower water and pour the liquid over the fruit. Cover and refrigerate for a couple of hours if you can.

5 Sift a little confectioner's sugar over the top immediately before serving.

FRUIT COUSCOUS WITH PRESERVED LEMON

I make fruit couscous all the time to serve with spiced fish, chicken or lamb. The preserved lemon provides a bass note that stops this dish from being just sweet and simple, making it something altogether more complex.

Serves 6 as a side dish

2¾ oz dried apricots

2oz raisins or sultanas

⅝ cup (5fl oz) orange juice

8oz couscous

⅞ cup (7fl oz) chicken or
   vegetable stock, or water

½ onion, finely chopped

1 tbsp olive oil

1 garlic clove, finely chopped

1 tsp mixed spice

salt and pepper

¼ preserved lemon, plus 1 tbsp
   of the preserved lemon
   juice (*see* p165)

3½ oz pistachios,
   roughly chopped

a small bunch of cilantro,
   roughly chopped

1 Cover the dried fruit in a mixture of orange juice and enough just boiled water to cover, and leave to soak. Sprinkle the couscous into a large flat container and pour half the stock or water over the top. Let the couscous plump up for about 15 minutes, then fork it through to separate the grains; repeat this with the rest of the liquid.

2 Sauté the onion in the olive oil until translucent. Add the garlic and mixed spice and cook for another minute.

3 Drain the fruits, chop the apricots, and stir them and the raisins into the couscous with the onion mix. Season and steam for 10 minutes. You don't need a steamer for this – put the couscous in a sieve lined with a clean dishcloth, set over a pan of simmering water, and cover the pan.

4 It's the rind of the preserved lemon that is used here, so cut away the fleshy bit and slice the remainder into fine slivers. These fruits provide a wonderful salty-sour Middle Eastern flavor, beautifully enhanced by the lemony juice in which they're preserved, but if you can't find them, and don't want to make your own, substitute the finely grated rind of ½ a fresh lemon and use some lemon-infused olive oil instead of the preserving juices. It will give you a different result, but you'll still have a sense of lemon.

5 Stir the lemon, the lemon juice, pistachios, and chopped cilantro into the warm couscous and serve.

"We open

the halves

of a miracle,

and a clotting of acids

brims

into the starry

divisions:

creation's

original juices…"

PABLO NERUDA, "A LEMON"

MIDDLE EASTERN ORANGE CAKE WITH MARMALADE AND ORANGE-FLOWER CREAM

I love making this. I'm so enthralled by the alchemy that can turn puréed boiled oranges into a sweet, moist cake. Pure culinary magic.

serves 8

1 orange

3 eggs

9oz superfine sugar

2oz all-purpose flour, sifted

1 tsp baking powder

7oz freshly ground almonds

confectioner's sugar for
dusting

FOR THE CREAM

2oz fine-shred
    orange marmalade

4½ oz mascarpone cheese

2 tbsp Greek yogurt

confectioner's sugar to taste

1 tsp orange-flower water

1 Put the orange in a saucepan, cover with water, and simmer for an hour. Cut the orange in half, remove the pips, and purée the rest of the fruit in a food processor.

2 Grease an eight-inch springform pan and line with baking parchment. Beat the eggs and sugar together until they're pale and thick. Fold in the flour, baking powder, almonds, and orange purée. Pour into the pan and bake in an oven preheated to 350°F for about an hour, or until a skewer inserted into the middle of the cake comes out clean. Turn the cake out to cool.

3 To make the cream, melt the marmalade in a small pan. Let it cool slightly, but don't let it set, then mix it with the mascarpone and yogurt. Add confectioner's sugar to taste and the orange-flower water.

4 Sift more confectioner's sugar over the cake, and serve with the marmalade cream.

"It is winter now ... but the oranges, tangerines, and lemons are all ripe; they burn in this clear atmosphere — the lemons with gentle flames, the tangerines with bright flashes, and the oranges sombre."

THE LETTERS OF KATHERINE MANSFIELD,
VOLUME ONE

MIDDLE EASTERN ORANGE CONFIT

This isn't a jam, but more of a Middle Eastern "spoon-sweet"– a rich preserve eaten as a treat, accompanied by glasses of water and cups of strong coffee. I like it with labneh, *rice pudding, and ice-cream as well.*

Makes about 3lb 5oz

2lb oranges, unwaxed and organic if possible

2lb superfine sugar

juice of 3 limes

freshly squeezed orange juice

water

3½fl oz orange-flower water (or less if you'd prefer it not so fragrant)

1 Wash the oranges, remove the rind with a vegetable peeler, and cut it into shreds as you would for marmalade. Put the rind into a small saucepan, cover with water and cook for 10 minutes. Drain.

2 Remove the white pith from the oranges and discard it. Slice the oranges finely, throwing away any pips, and put the slices into a large saucepan with the rind. Add the sugar, lime juice, and enough orange juice and water – half of each – to just cover the flesh. Add the orange-flower water. Bring the mixture up to the boil slowly, stirring to help dissolve the sugar. Turn the heat down and simmer everything for an hour. Cover the pan and leave it overnight.

3 Next day heat the mixture again and simmer it for 20-30 minutes (the length of time will depend on the size of your saucepan) until it is quite thick and syrupy. This is not a jam so it will not reach a setting point.

4 Put into clean jars. Store in the refrigerator. It keeps for about eight weeks.

AMALFI LEMON AND HONEY JAM

You see pots of this for sale all over the Amalfi coast. I thought it was such a lovely idea, I came home and made my own.

Makes about 3lb 5oz

2lb unwaxed lemons

5 cups (40fl oz) water

1½lb clear honey

2¾lb preserving sugar

1 Wash the lemons and cut off the rind, removing and reserving any pith. Slice the peel into fine julienne strips. Cut the flesh roughly, ensuring no juice is lost, and removing and reserving any pith or pips. Put the pith and pips into cheesecloth. Tie it up and put it into a saucepan with the flesh, juice, and rind.

2 Add the water and simmer for 1½ hours. Remove the cheesecloth bag, squeezing it over the pan. Add the honey and sugar and, over a low heat, stir everything until the sugar has dissolved. Boil rapidly until the setting point is reached: test by putting a spoonful of the jam on a cold saucer. If, after a minute, the jam wrinkles when you push it, it is ready. Allow the jam to cool a little, then put it into sterilized jars. Seal once the jam is cold.

RUBY GRAPEFRUIT AND CAMPARI GRANITA

This is a very grown-up, cleansing end to a meal and an easy one. With granitas there's no messing about with custards or ice-cream machines — just sweet liquid, a freezer and a fork. Pile the bittersweet crystals into chilled glasses and leave it at that. If you're feeling particularly lazy, use a bottle of freshly squeezed juice.

serves 4-6

2¼ cups (18fl oz) freshly
   squeezed ruby
   grapefruit juice

5½ oz superfine sugar

5 tbsp Campari

1 Gently heat the juice with the superfine sugar until the sugar has melted. Leave to cool. Add the Campari and then pour the liquid into a wide shallow container and put it into the freezer.

2 After about an hour, fork the crystals forming round the edges into the rest of the juice. Keep doing this at intervals, forking the slush to break it up as it freezes. You want to end up with fine, glassy shards of ice.

3 If the mixture sets hard, just leave it out for 5 minutes and fork it again before serving.

"The train drew into Catania…

'I want a granita, *a* granita *and some biscuits,' said Nene. 'Me, too. I want a* granita *and some brioches,' said Lulu.*

They had granita, *biscuits, and brioches. 'They call this stuff* granita?' *said Nene disgustedly, but only when he had drained (partly on his clothes) the last mushy drop. 'Don Pasqualino makes real* granita. *As soon as we get to Nisimia, I shall drink a bucketful!'"*

LEONARDO SCIASCIA, *THE WINE-DARK SEA*

"At this stage the attendants produced graceful perfume-bottles, some full of rose water, and some of orange-blossom lotion, jessamine, and extract of citron-blooms..."

GIOVANNI BOCCACCIO, *THE DECAMERON*

HEAVEN SCENT

FLOWERS AND FLOWER WATERS

I fell for the idea of eating flowers when I was six. At a school rummage sale there was a raffle for a cake. It was tiered, covered in thick, creamy-white icing, and adorned with a cascade of fragrant, deep-red rose petals and half-closed buds. I was mesmerized – this was a cake for Snow White – and I couldn't fill my nostrils enough with its scent. I felt like the only way to capture this smell was to eat the cake. But we didn't win the raffle. Someone else carried away the promise of consuming those velvet flowers. By chance, the present bought to ease this disappointment was my first bottle of perfume – a little china capsule of African violets. I kept sniffing it. I could taste the smell and I really wanted to eat its purpleness.

For many people, the idea of flowers and their fragrance conjures up images of an English afternoon tea – a sweet little cake dotted with crystallized petals to match the china cups – or the musty corners of granny's handbag. The whole notion is cosy, cute, even a little cloying. Not me. I have always felt that the subtlety of petals and their scent rendered them uncapturable and hence mysterious, foreign, and desirable. I couldn't devour those violets the way I would a chocolate bar, and I wanted to.

As far as violets go, I was right – their smell is literally evanescent. Violets contain ionine, a chemical that temporarily short-circuits our sense of smell, so their fragrance comes and goes in bursts. You can't drink in the scent the way you want to. But roses and orange blossom seem ephemeral, too. That is the magic of floral smells. Your nose can follow them like your eyes would follow a piece of silk as it darts through a network of alleyways. When you taste them, the flavor still eludes you, as if you are eating a piece of a place that might not exist, or a memory of something that never really happened. And I'm not the only one who feels like this – few things over the centuries have tantalized and seduced like scents. The ancient Persians made wine from rose petals, the Romans strewed their floors with them, Cleopatra anointed her hands with oil of roses, crocus, and violets, and Napoleon, even during his toughest campaigns, took time to choose between rose- and violet-scented finery. Forget Granny's cupboards – think Anthony and Cleopatra making love on a bed of petals, Roman diners being sprayed with flower waters between courses, and gladiators rubbing oil of flowers into their loins.

Now, in an age when the most exotic spices have been made familiar by supermarkets and take-outs, the smell of blossoms in our saucepans is one of the few scents that can still really transport us. Both rose water and orange-flower water are used all over the Middle East and North Africa. Pastries are drenched in scented sugar syrups and rose petal jam is eaten at breakfast or as a spoon-sweet served at afternoon tea with tinkling silver spoons, cups of strong coffee and little glasses of iced water.

A tablespoon of orange-flower water stirred into a cup of boiling water is known as a *café blanc* in the Lebanon, and drops of flower water added to Persian fruit and meat stews – *khoresht* – lend them a haunting, indefinable flavor. Dried rose petals are part of the Persian spice mix *advieh*, in which they join cinnamon, cardamom, and cumin, and are also added to the classic North African spice blend *ras al hanout*. You'd think the blossoms' flavor would be lost among these powerful competitors, but they add a delicate, sweet muskiness.

Flowers have been used for years to flavor *sharbats*, the sugary syrups that are the base of cold drinks made all over the Arab world. As Claudia Roden writes in *New Book of Middle Eastern Food*, remembering the cries of the *sharbat* vendors in the Cairo of her childhood: "The vendors carried a selection of sherbets in gigantic glass flasks … The flasks glowed with brilliantly seductive colors: soft, pale, sugary pink for rose water; pale green for violet juice; warm, rich, dark tamarind and the purple-black of mulberry juice."

No one is certain whether it was Arab *sharbats* that eventually metamorphosed into the ice creams of Naples and Sicily but, when the Arabs were in power, snow was brought from Etna to ice these drinks. Perhaps it wasn't much of a leap from near-frozen *sharbat* to *granita* and, eventually, sorbet. In any case, you can still find orange-blossom and jasmine ice creams in Sicily, and Middle Eastern ice cream flavored with rose water is one of the most sublime tastes in the world – it's just subtle enough to be like eating spoonfuls of a summer that is past.

The great thing is that these drops of exotica are quite attainable. Middle Eastern and Indian groceries stock orange-flower water, made from the blossom of the Seville orange, and rose water, and it's not difficult to get hold of a handful of fragrant rose petals.

American chef Jerry Traunfeld, who cooks at The Herbfarm restaurant near Seattle, specializes in cooking with herbs and flowers. He makes floral syrups by whizzing petals and sugar in a food processor before adding water and boiling to a sticky, limpid liquid. These are used for fruit salads and as a base for sorbets. The sugars last for ages – just keep them in a screwtop jar and add them to whipped cream or fruit fools, sift over fruit-topped meringues, or use them in cake batter or to make a butter-cream filling.

All rose petals, as long as they haven't been sprayed with pesticides, are quite edible, but they differ enormously in their smell and taste. The modern hybrid tea roses have been bred for form rather than for fragrance, so use the old-fashioned, flat, full, blossoming roses, which are much more heady. If you're going to make rose jam, or something that needs a lot of rose petals, it is best to either befriend a sympathetic gardener or to grow them yourself, but you can impart enough rose fragrance to most things with flower water or, if they're heavily scented enough, a few blooms. Try throwing a handful of petals over the fruit in a cherry pie before baking it, or making a punch from a bottle of rosé Champagne, a little cassis, and a slug of rose water; float strawberries and rose petals on top and you have a drink that could be served at the wedding feast in *A Midsummer Night's Dream*.

Rose water has a wonderful affinity with red summer fruits, but try using it as they do in the Middle East, too – add it to poached apples in the winter, or chilled, grated apples or melon in the summer. Both rose water and orange-flower water transport milk puddings: a little orange water and a few pods of crushed cardamom can take a plain old rice pudding to the shores of the Bosphorous in one delicious mouthful.

Orange-flower water tastes good with golden-colored fruits – peaches, nectarines, mangoes, and apricots – and really enhances almonds, so stick it into cakes, tarts, and cookies for a little perfume of Provence, where it's also popular. Use a lighter hand than you do with rose water or it can become rather sickly, though to be honest I could drink the stuff. I can never smell orange-flower water without simultaneously smelling the scents of fresh mint and sweat – the smell of Arab markets. If you like smells for their power to transport you, orange water is a rocket. When I've been baking a lot with it, scattering it over little Arab pastries, my kitchen and my skin breathe Morocco.

Violets are much more English and much less versatile. They're used for those violet fondant creams so beloved of the Queen Mother, but they don't turn up much in the Middle East. The French have a penchant for them, though. In Toulouse they've been growing the heavily scented Parma violets since the 1850s, turning them into jam – the delicate petals suspended in a translucent mauve jelly – and, of course, crystallizing the heads. There's even a violet liqueur that looks wickedly purple but smells innocently sweet. The jam and the crystallized flowers are easy to pick up in specialist food stores in France, but you'll have to find an enterprising food emporium or specialist spirit importer for the liqueur.

The smell of violets is certainly more cloying than that of orange blossom or roses, the kind of overly-sweet scent that schoolgirls fall for – in fact, I used to stand in my school uniform in the sweet shop, passing my allowance from one hot hand to the other, torn between the perfumed romance of a packet of Parma Violets (a cellophane-wrapped tube of lilac-colored buttons) and the adult sophistication of a bar of Fry's Chocolate Cream. It's a shame that you couldn't have mixed the two: the taste of violets is wonderful with both white and dark chocolate. Try adding a few drops of violet liqueur to the glaze or filling for a chocolate cake. Violets are good with strawberries, raspberries, and apricots, too. Wines made from the Viognier grape are often described as having the scents of both violets and apricots, so I suppose that the pairing isn't really surprising. Add just a dash of violet liqueur to the syrup in which you have poached apricots, or to a bowl of cream to be served alongside.

Using flowers in food won't be to everyone's taste, but the power scents have to evoke memories and a sense of place makes them an irresistible ingredient. A couple of bottles of flower water and a few handfuls of petals will turn you into a *parfumier* as well as a cook, with the art of catering for the most complex of senses as well as the most basic.

MERINGUE AND ROSE CAKE WITH SUMMER BERRIES

With its creamy-white tiers and scattering of rose petals, this is a great wedding dress of a cake whose extravagant appearance belies its simplicity. It really is a case of maximum visual impact for minimum effort – a perfect combination of a pretty English garden and the magic of The Arabian Nights.

serves 12

FOR THE MERINGUES

9 egg whites

1lb 2oz superfine sugar

FOR THE FILLING

3¼ cups (26fl oz)
    whipping cream

3½ fl oz Greek yogurt

9 tbsp confectioner's sugar

6 tbsp rose water, or to taste

14oz strawberries

10½ oz raspberries

5½ oz redcurrants (or other
    berry of your choice)

5½ oz blueberries

FOR THE TOPPING

petals from 2 fragrant roses

2 egg whites, very lightly
    beaten (optional)

sifted superfine sugar (optional)

1 If you're going to crystallize the rose petals for the topping, simply paint each one with egg white and then dip in superfine sugar, making sure that it gets well-coated. Set on a wire cooling rack and leave somewhere warm and dry to harden. It will take about 1½ hours.

2 To make the meringues, beat the egg whites until stiff, then add half the sugar. Whisk again until the mixture is very glossy, then add the rest of the sugar and beat lightly to incorporate.

3 Line several baking sheets with baking parchment. Spoon onto one sheet a flat disk shape of egg whites, measuring 10½ inches in diameter. On another sheet, spoon out a flat disk of about eight inches. On a third sheet, spoon out an unflattened disk of about five inches) and put a turret of egg white on top. Bake in an oven preheated to 225°F for 2 hours. The meringues should be dry and lift off the paper easily. Leave to cool.

4 For the filling, lightly whip the cream, then fold in the yogurt, sugar, and rose water. Layer the meringue disks with the cream mixture and fruit, making sure that you allow some of the fruits to peek out at the sides.

5 If you're using crystallized petals dot them all over the cake, tucking them in or using cream as a glue. You can't just throw them nonchalantly, however enchanting that notion may be, as they just fall off. On the other hand, if you feel like going for wanton romance (which, after all, is the point of this cake), throw fresh petals over the top and hope that they fall beautifully.

" ...I was haunted by the memory of a cake. It used to float in the air before me – a delicate thing stuffed *with cream and with the cream there was something* scarlet *... I used to call it my* Arabian Nights *cake..."*

THE LETTERS OF KATHERINE MANSFIELD, VOL ONE

TURKISH ROSE ICE CREAM

This is like eating iced Turkish delight. Substitute cornstarch if you can't get hold of salep *(a starch made from dried, powdered orchid tubers), but do try to find it in Turkish or Middle Eastern stores first (you should find mastic there, too). It gives the ice cream a strange elasticity.*

Serves 6-8

3 tbsp *salep*

2 cups (16fl oz) milk

⅛ tsp mastic

⅝ cup (5fl oz) heavy cream

4½ oz superfine sugar

3 tbsp rose water

1 Mix the *salep* with a little of the milk. Grind the mastic in a mortar and pestle until fine (you might find you need to add a little granulated sugar to act as an abrasive). Heat the rest of the milk with the cream and sugar, stirring to help the sugar dissolve. Add the *salep* and milk mixture and bring to the boil. Tip in the mastic. Turn the heat down and let everything simmer for 10 minutes, stirring from time to time.

2 Let this cool, then add the rose water. Churn in an ice-cream machine, or still-freeze, beating the cream in a food processor two or three times during the freezing process.

NIÇOIS CARNIVAL FRITTERS

Les ganses in French, these little fritters are eaten at Mardi Gras in Nice. I love making them — it always seems so celebratory waiting around for them to cook, then eating them hot, showered with sugar. Serve them with coffee or dessert wine.

serves 4-6

4½ oz all-purpose flour

½ tsp baking powder

1½ tbsp superfine sugar

a pinch of salt

3½ oz all-purpose flour

finely grated rind of 1 orange

1½ oz butter, melted & cooled

1 egg, beaten

1 tbsp milk

½ tbsp orange-flower water

groundnut (peanut) oil
   for deep-frying

confectioner's sugar
   for dusting

1 Sift the dry ingredients into a large bowl. Make a well in the center and add the rind, butter and egg. Bring the flour into the well and mix everything together. Add the milk and the flower water and form the dough into a ball. Let it rest for half an hour.

2 Roll out the dough to ¹⁄₁₆-inch thickness and cut it into strips, about ⅝ inch wide and six inches long. Tie these into loose knots, drop them into hot oil, and fry until deep-golden in color. Drain on paper towels and dust immediately with confectioner's sugar.

ROSE-SCENTED RHUBARB WITH RIZOGALO

Rizogalo is Greek rice pudding — rich yet light and quick to cook since it's done on the stove-top. I also serve it in the winter with poached plums or a salad of sliced citrus fruits in a tangy, sweet syrup. The mastic does impart a particular flavor, but if you can't get hold of it, just leave it out. You could also try the dish with a little flower water added to the rice instead of the fruit.

serves 4-6

1lb 5oz rhubarb, trimmed and
    cut into (3½in) lengths

5½oz superfine sugar

⅝ cup (5fl oz) water

1 tbsp rose water, or to taste

chopped pistachios or plain or
    crystallized rose petals
    to serve

FOR THE RICE

2½oz short-grain rice

3⅔ cups (30fl oz) whole milk

2oz superfine sugar

¼ tsp mastic, ground in a mortar

1 egg yolk

4 tbsp thick heavy cream

1 Put the rice in a saucepan and cover it with water. Bring the water up to the boil and cook the rice for 4 minutes. Remove the pan from the heat and drain the rice. Put the rice back in the pan with the milk, sugar, and mastic, bring to the boil, and then turn down to a very gentle simmer. Cook gently until all the liquid is absorbed — it takes about 15 minutes and you need to stir from time to time. Take the pan off the heat. Mix the egg yolk with the cream, then stir this into the rice. In order to cool the rice more quickly, tip it into a bowl.

2 Put the rhubarb into an ovenproof dish, then add the sugar and water. Cover with foil and bake in a preheated oven at 350°F for 30-40 minutes (it really depends on the thickness of your rhubarb, so do check it). You want to end up with tender but not stewed rhubarb.

3 Carefully drain the rhubarb of its juice and set it aside. Bring the fruit juice to the boil and simmer until it becomes syrupy. Let it cool, then add the rose water.

4 Serve the rhubarb and rice in two large separate bowls, or together in individual soup plates, garnished with rose petals or pistachios.

"After Matisse:

picnics beneath olive trees;

the Sunday light cuts shadows

like painted paper...

Beignets, Socca, Bagne Cauda:

tastes bright as bougainvillea..."

ADRIAN HENRI, *APROPOS DE NICE*

ICE IN HEAVEN

You just can't resist a dessert with a name like this. Scented with roses and served in little glasses or cups, it really is rather celestial. In its Middle Eastern home, it's made with even more sugar, but I've reduced this and added the berries to cut through the sweetness; use a few for decoration and serve the rest in a bowl.

serves 4

2oz ground rice

½oz) blanched almonds, freshly ground

1½oz superfine sugar

1⅝ cups (13fl oz) milk

3 tbsp whipping cream

2 tbsp rose water

juice of ½ lime

5½oz mixed berries (choose from raspberries, blackberries, blueberries, etc)

a handful of fresh or crystallized rose petals

1 Put the rice, almonds, sugar, and milk into a heavy-bottomed saucepan. Heat slowly, while stirring with a wooden spoon, until the mixture thickens and bubbles gently. Turn down the heat and continue to cook and stir the mixture for another 5 minutes. If you find the mixture gets very thick, you can add more milk.

2 Add the cream, rose water, and lime juice and taste – you may want to add a little more of any of these.

3 Spoon the rice into separate little glasses and allow to cool.

4 Serve the dessert really well-chilled, scattered with berries and rose petals. You can leave the latter whole, tear them or cut them into little shreds like confetti.

"Look to the rose that blows about us – 'Lo Laughing,'

she says, 'into the World I blow':

At once the silken Tassel of my Purse

Tear, and its Treasure on the

Garden throw."

THE RUBAIYAT OF OMAR KHAYYAM

HOW TO DRY ROSE LEAVES IN A MOST EXCELLENT MANNER

WHEN you have newly taken out your bread, then put in your Roses in a sieve, first clipping away the whites that they may be all of one colour, lay them about one inch in thickness in the sieve; and when they have stood halfe an houre, or thereabout, they will grow whitish on the top; let them yet remaine without stirring, till the upper-most of them bee fully dried: then stirre them together, and leave them about one other halfe houre, and if you finde them dry in the top, stirre them together againe, and so continue this worke about three or four times, then put them hot in a dry box; or being dryed within a day or two, as you shall finde it, put them hot into a glasse, and stop it, and after a while they will purfume as well the [illegible] ... and this so will keep them [illegible] ...

ROSE AND APPLE JELLY

Rose petals alone are used for making this jam in the Middle East (it's sometimes eaten with drained yogurt and bread for breakfast), but it's difficult to get it to set as rose petals have no pectin. Apples have loads of pectin, and are a really good partner for roses, carrying their fragrance without overwhelming it. Try to get heavily scented roses and be prepared to judge the amount of rose water you need to add once the jam is near setting point.

If making this doesn't make you feel like an eastern goddess, nothing will, though spreading it on warm scones — my usual use for it — will bring you gently down to earth again. Keep it in the refrigerator once it's opened.

makes about 1¼ lb

2¾ lb cooking apples

juice of 1 lime

7oz scented rose petals

superfine sugar

3 tbsp rose water, or to taste

TO FINISH

extra rose petals,
  carefully washed

1 Roughly chop the apples, without peeling or coring, and put them into a preserving pan or large saucepan with 3½ cups (28fl oz) water and the lime juice. Simmer for about 40 minutes until very soft and mushy. Spoon this into a jelly bag and leave it suspended to drain for at least 12 hours.

2 Put the petals in a saucepan with 7fl oz water, cover and simmer for 15 minutes. Leave to infuse for a couple of hours, then strain.

3 Mix the rose liquid and the liquid from the apples together and measure. For every 2½ cups (20 fl oz) juice add 12oz superfine sugar. Heat gently, stirring to help the sugar dissolve, then bring the liquid up to the boil. Boil rapidly until the setting point is reached, skimming any scum off the top. To gauge whether you have reached setting point, put a teaspoonful of the liquid on a cold saucer. If, after a minute, you can push this with your finger and it wrinkles, the jelly is ready. Add the rose water.

4 While still warm, spoon the jelly into sterilized jars, adding some more rose petals to each one, and cover the surface with a waxed paper disk. When the jelly is quite cold, put the lids on the jars.

"...there is poetry in making preserves; the housewife has caught duration in the snare of sugar, she has enclosed life in jars."

SIMONE DE BEAUVOIR, THE SECOND SEX

POACHED PRUNES WITH ROSE WATER CREAM

This dish was born of indecision. I couldn't make up my mind whether to cook Claudia Roden's recipe for Walnut Stuffed Prunes in her Book of Middle Eastern Food, or to just serve pitted prunes stuffed with dark chocolate, as I'd had them in Italy. In the end I did an amalgamation of both, adding the very un-Middle Eastern touches of wine and cassis. Too much gilding of the lily, you might think, but I love this dish, even though a little goes a long way. I used to stuff each prune with a walnut and a nugget of chocolate, but it was a sticky and laborious affair, so now I do a lazy version — without any effect whatsoever on the taste.

serves 6

8oz pitted prunes

⅝ cup (5fl oz) red wine

⅝ cup (5fl oz) cold tea
  (preferably a perfumed one)

3 tbsp superfine sugar

1½ tbsp cassis

1½ oz shelled walnuts, toasted
  and chopped

2oz good-quality dark
  (semi-sweet) chocolate,
  partly chopped and
  partly grated

a handful of crystallized or
  fresh edible rose petals,
  or chopped
toasted walnuts, for serving

FOR THE CREAM

⅝ cup (5fl oz) whipping cream

5½ fl oz Greek yogurt

3 tbsp confectioner's sugar

3 tbsp rose water

2 tbsp cassis

1 Put the prunes in a saucepan with the red wine, tea, sugar, and cassis. Bring slowly to the boil, stirring from time to time to help the sugar melt. Turn the heat down and simmer the prunes for about 20 minutes. You should be left with a small amount of thick syrup. Let the prunes cool in the liquid.

2 Put the prunes and their syrup in a serving bowl, or divide among four little glasses to serve individually. Scatter the walnuts and chocolate over the top of the prunes.

3 Lightly whip the cream and mix it with all the other cream ingredients. Spoon over the prunes and leave for a few hours before serving. This is also delicious the next day. Strew the top with either crystallized or fresh rose petals or toasted walnuts just before dishing it up.

"He would now study perfumes, and the secrets of their manufacture, distilling heavily scented oils, and burning odorous gums from the East. He saw that there was no mood of the mind that had not its counterpart in the sensuous life, and set himself to discover their true relation, wondering what there was in frankincense that made one mystical, and in ambergris that stirred one's passions, and in violets that woke the memory of dead romance..."

OSCAR WILDE, *THE PICTURE OF DORIAN GRAY*

MANGOES WITH ORANGE-BLOSSOM SYRUP AND SWEET LABNEH

Labneh *is nothing more than a firm white cloud of drained Greek yogurt, but it makes a great base for simple, striking-looking desserts.*

serves 4

3 just ripe mangoes

finely chopped pistachios
    for serving

FOR THE LABNEH

1½ tbsp confectioner's sugar

a pinch of ground cinnamon

10½ fl oz Greek yogurt

FOR THE SYRUP

6 tbsp orange-blossom honey

3 tbsp orange juice

a good squeeze of lime juice

1½ tbsp orange-flower water

1 Add the sugar and cinnamon to the yogurt, put into a sieve lined with cheesecloth, and set it over a bowl. Let the yogurt drain for 24 hours, giving it a little help every so often by picking up the bag and squeezing it.

2 To make the syrup, gently heat the honey, orange, and lime juices together in a small saucepan. Once the honey has melted, boil for 1 minute. Add the orange-flower water and taste. Leave to cool.

3 Peel the mangoes and, using a really sharp knife, neatly slice the cheeks from each side of the stone. Working along the shape of the stone, slice the flesh off the sides. Cut the mango flesh into neat slices, about ⅛-¼ inch thick, and pile them on top of each other on different plates.

4 Peel the cheesecloth from around the *labneh*, then divide it into quarters. It isn't important, but the cheesecloth leaves such beautiful markings on the *labneh* that it's nice not to spoil it. Put a chunk of *labneh* beside each pile of mangoes, spoon the syrup over the top, and scatter with pistachios.

FLOWER-SCENTED TRUFFLES

I adore those flower-scented fondant chocolates so loved by Britain's Queen Mother, but making fondant is a bit of a messy and exacting job, so this is my, rather easier, substitute. Professionals manage to coat chocolates without letting a "foot" form beneath each one. I never manage this, but there's nothing wrong with your chocolates looking homemade. After all, you wouldn't want to go to all that trouble and have people think you bought them! Look for violet liqueur in a specialist wine or liquor store. There are several French versions available.

VIOLET LIQUEUR TRUFFLES

Makes 16 truffles

7oz white chocolate, broken
    into pieces
4 tbsp crème fraîche
    (or sour cream)
3 tbsp violet liqueur
confectioner's sugar
    for shaping
5½oz dark (semi-sweet)
    chocolate for coating,
    broken into pieces
crystallized violets
    for decoration

1 Melt the white chocolate in a bowl set over a pan of simmering water. Stir in the crème fraîche and mix well. Add the liqueur. Stir and let the mixture cool, then put it in the refrigerator to firm up – it will take 3-4 hours.

2 Once the chocolate is cool and firm, scoop up walnut-sized pieces of it. Roll lightly in sifted confectioner's sugar and refrigerate again. The truffles need to be really chilled and firm to withstand being coated.

3 When the truffles are ready, melt the dark chocolate in a bowl over a pan of simmering water. With a pronged, long-handled fork, roll each truffle in the chocolate until coated. Lift it out on the prongs – but do not pierce it – and shake off the excess chocolate by tapping the neck of the fork against the side of the bowl. Do this a couple more times and tap the neck of the fork until no more chocolate drips off.

4 Tip each truffle onto waxed paper and decorate with the crystallized violets. Leave the truffles to cool a little and set. Because of the cream content they need to be stored in the refrigerator and eaten within 48 hours.

ROSE TRUFFLES

Make in the same way as above, adding 1 tbsp rose water and the juice of half a lime to the cream mixture instead of the violet liqueur. Decorate with crystallized rose petals.

RECIPE INDEX
BY INGREDIENT